LISTENING TO THE BEAT OF OUR DRUM

Funded by the Government of Canada
Financé par la gouvernement du Canada

Demeter Press
140 Holland Street West
P. O. Box 13022
Bradford, ON L3Z 2Y5
Tel: (905) 775-9089
Email: info@demeterpress.org
Website: www.demeterpress.org

Demeter Press logo based on the sculpture “Demeter” by Maria-Luise Bodirsky <www.keramik-atelier.bodirsky.de>

Front cover artwork: Leah Marie Dorion, “Two Drums Become One,”2014, acrylic on canvas, 40 x 36 inches. www.leahdorion.ca

Printed and Bound in Canada

Library and Archives Canada Cataloguing in Publication

Listening to the beat of our drum : stories of indigenous parenting in contemporary society / edited by Carrie Bourassa, elder Betty McKenna, and Darlene Juschka.

Includes bibliographical references and index.
ISBN 978-1-77258-106-5 (softcover)

1. Indian mothers. 2. Parenting. 3. Motherhood. I. Bourassa, Carrie A., 1973-, editor II. McKenna, Betty, 1949-, editor III. Juschka, Darlene, 1957-, editor

HQ759.L57 2017 306.874’308997 C2017-902196-6

LISTENING TO THE BEAT OF OUR DRUM

Indigenous Parenting in Contemporary Society

EDITED BY

Carrie Bourassa, Elder Betty McKenna and Darlene Juschka

DEMETER PRESS

For my Gramps who was my mother, my father, my rock. I miss you every day. You are always in my heart, and I take you everywhere I go. I would not be the mother that I am without you. Thank you for the lessons you taught me and continue to teach me from the Spirit World.

For my husband, who is the most amazing parent to our two beautiful children. You are the most incredible role model.

To my reason for being, my daughters—Victoria, La Tete Ayikis Quay (Head Frog Woman), and Lillie, Pisim Asikinak (Sun Turtle). Thank you for choosing me to be your mother.

For my kookum, my mentor, Elder Betty McKenna, I can never thank you enough for the teachings and guidance you provide to me and my family. Love you always.

— Carrie Bourassa

To my family, who have supported me in all my endeavours.

—Elder Betty McKenna

Table of Contents

Acknowledgements

Carrie Bourassa would like to thank Elder Betty McKenna for her prayers, guidance, and immense contributions to this book.

A huge thank you, also, to Ashley Landers and Dr. Darlene Juschka for their editing assistance and the many hours they put into this project. Much love and respect to you both.

Thank you to Dr. Blair Stonechild for his thoughtful contribution and guidance.

Foreword

BLAIR STONECHILD

THE BOOK *Listening to the Beat of Our Drum: Indigenous Parenting in a Contemporary Society* is an important contribution in these times of Truth and Reconciliation and cultural revitalization. The inescapable effect that colonialism has wreaked upon Indigenous families' and Indigenous people's own perceptions of gender roles is impossible to ignore. Every day, one hears about the legacy of colonization and residential schools in the news when one reads about impoverishment, Indigenous youth crime, family violence and so forth. Parenting, once so valued in traditional societies, has become a real challenge for Indigenous parents seeking cultural integrity and to raise their children with values difficult to maintain in today's materialistic society.

The stories in *Listening to the Beat of Our Drum: Indigenous Parenting in a Contemporary Society* are heartfelt accounts of such personal experiences. As the originator of the idea for the book, Carrie Bourassa reflects in her own life and experiences with gender, both good and bad. For Carrie, the discussion of parenting from an Indigenous perspective is the fulfillment of a lifelong dream. Elder Betty McKenna contributes an important and often-overlooked bit of wisdom that "our warriors will come full circle so that mothering will once again not be separated by gender." She brings attention to the issue of Indigenous masculinity and the need for males to rediscover the sensitivity toward relationships that made them traditionally strong. Gender studies professor Darlene Juschka contributes important historical, colonialist, and feminist perspectives to the discussion.

Contributors Janet Smylie and Nancy Cooper write about navigating the complexities of life within a two-spirited relationship. Paulette Poitras describes how her supportive family relationships have strengthened Indigenous identity and have given her courage. Tara Turner reflects on her struggle to recover her Metis identity and the implications when it comes to raising children. All authors reflect in their own way on how the recovery of Indigenous cultural and gender identity has affected their lives and how they now live.

The issue of gender is one mired in the detritus of history. As Indigenous spiritual, cultural, and social systems were ground down by the relentless march of "progress," Indigenous males and females had to increasingly adopt Euro-American gender roles to survive. The overwhelming of the Americas by militarized invaders left the unfortunate impression that power and money would resolve all issues and everyone would live "happily ever after." The problem is spiritual imbalance, which has taken centuries to manifest itself. The disrespect for the spirit in nonhuman creation has left us with a legacy of resource depletion, climate change, poisoned water, species extinction, and increasing human violence.

The attitudes of patriarchy and power, which have come to mark modern life, are reflected in contemporary male-female roles. Several scholars have pointed out how the effects of colonialism have broken the gender balance and respect that once existed between the genders. Indigenous cultures recognize that each gender has unique and legitimate roles to play in creation. Ceremonies also reinforce respect for these relationships and brought healing when these cultural relationships were abused.

A number of the contributors refer to the importance of spirituality and ceremonies. From my perspective of having worked with elders during my tenure at First Nations University of Canada in Regina, Saskatchewan, and having just completed the book *The Knowledge Seeker: Embracing Indigenous Spirituality*, I believe I can offer some useful comments.

First, it is not adequately recognized that pre-Contact Indigenous societies valued spirituality above all else. It is impossible to appreciate how Indigenous peoples lived and behaved without understanding their spiritual philosophies and practices. In Indigenous culture, being consists of four elements: the physical, emotional, intellectual, and spiritual. As I have been taught by elder mentors, Indigenous cultures viewed the spiritual component of being as the most important and having a very real impact.

My mentor, the distinguished Elder Danny Musqua, has stated that as humans, we are really spirit beings who came to the world and will return to spirit after death. Our bodies are simply vehicles that we use as we transit through a constantly changing and impermanent physical environment. Humans who express the desire to experience the physical world, however, make a major sacrifice in doing so, which is the separation into physical bodies and egos. Our great challenge on Earth, then, is to overcome that separation through discovering our appropriate relationships, not only with other humans but also with all created things. In doing this, we fulfill our spiritual challenge.

Residential school survivors have experienced firsthand the effects of having their culture and identity stripped away from them and the confusion and emptiness that this experience left them with. I can personally attest to the schools' effectiveness in obliterating knowledge of our spirituality. Indigenous parents, especially those living in an urban environment, know what a tremendous challenge it is to instill traditional knowledge and practices in the lives of children who are constantly bombarded with messages about materialism and status. Elders are extremely concerned about the effects of loss of culture and spirituality among youth, who are increasingly engaging in substance abuse, crime, and gang involvement, and committing suicide. And families who have a missing or murdered female relative know the fallout from damaged gender relations.

Overall, the authors in this volume share meaningful reflections on their experiences in the hope that this will make it easier for others who face similar challenges. I feel that all inhabitants of contemporary North America are the victims of the unfortunate legacy of Indigenous cultural genocide and rape of the environment. However, as colonized populations, Indigenous people have the fewest resources and least power to do anything about it. I urge readers to listen to the stories told in *Listening to the Beat of Our Drum: Indigenous Parenting in a Contemporary Society* and take its message to heart for the sake of our future generations.

Introduction

CARRIE BOURASSA AND DARLENE JUSCHKA

LISTENING TO THE BEAT of Our Drum: Indigenous Parenting in a Contemporary Society is a labour of love. I am sure many authors and scholars alike have said this and it may sound like a cliché, but for me I cannot find another way to express my feelings. When my *kookum* (grandmother) Betty and I began talking about the possibility of a book, we started from spirit, that is, with ceremony. We started from love. Our love of each other, our love of our family, kin, ancestors, Mother Earth; indeed, All Our Relations as we often say. We hoped that this book would be read in classrooms to enrich and challenge eager minds and by all who seek to know more about mothering, relationships, parenting, soul searching, growth and, yes, tough issues such as colonization, loss, and reclamation. This book was inspired by a wealth of experiences across space and time but you, the reader, will see that the authors in this text share some of the life experiences of Indigenous parenting, and they hope their stories will resonate with you. In this book, you will hear experiences from a kookum, an auntie, two-spirit parents, a Métis mother, and me.

I am *Ts'iotaat Kutx Ayanaha s'eek* (Morning Star Bear). I am Tlingit/Anishinaabe Métis. My unique experience is that I had a very strong bond with my grandfather (or as I called him, gramps). He was not only my grandfather, as I saw him in many ways as both my father and mother. He took on those roles for me over the years until he passed when I was nineteen. It was and remains the greatest sorrow of my life. I still mourn his passing, and although it was twenty-four years ago, it still feels like yesterday.

My mother and father were teen parents, and we had a difficult relationship. Intergenerational trauma, addictions, and violence remained a constant from childhood throughout adulthood. I have no blame for them. These kinds of struggle are an unfortunate reality in many families, but it is magnified in Indigenous families as a result of the impacts of colonization.

My gramps was my rock as I always called him. He quit drinking when I was very young—so young that I never remember him drinking alcohol. He took ill when I was around nine years old, but he remained my primary caregiver and worked when he could. He instilled me with values and morals, and shared stories from his childhood that no one else was interested in. But I was. I cherished those stories. I cherished every single word he said. He is the sole reason I am still here. I know this deep in the core of my being. So many times I tried to run away, but the only reason I stayed was because of him. He was a kind and gentle man despite having been horribly abused as a child himself. He carried guilt and shame associated with his identity that resulted from his childhood, and he feared for me. He wanted me to grow up and become a doctor or a lawyer.

One time when I was about four years old, I was sitting on his lap in the kitchen. Everyone was drunk except for him, while my grandmother was also very intoxicated. I don't think I saw her sober more than five times in my entire life, and she passed away when I was thirty years old. My grandmother was starting to get violent, and I was getting a bit nervous. My gramps was gently whispering to me and telling me I would be safe. But he said something else—he said, "My girl, you will be the one to stop this. You are going to grow up to be a doctor or a lawyer. You do not want to be like this. You hear me?" I would get that lecture many times. It stuck with me, and I never wanted to let that man down.

Identity loss was a huge issue in our family—self-hatred, denial, and preservation meant hiding our Métis status. "It was a very tough time to be a half-breed family," he would say. That's what his family was labelled, and he recalled only avoiding racial slurs and taunts when he joined the Air Force. He could see that status made a difference, and he desperately wanted that for me. He would often tell me to try hard to fit in. Despite that, I had a tough time in school anyways with bullying and taunts—squaw, half-breed, you name it, and I was called it.

I was a naturally gifted student, yet when I might have veered off the path when I got older while I was bouncing between my gramps's house and my mother and father's house—trading an environment of my grandmother's alcohol addiction for my mother's drug addiction—my gramps was always there for me. I recall many times his coming to get me and taking me to his house—somehow he just knew when I needed to be with him. He had an amazing sense of humour and was always playing pranks on me and making me laugh. The resilience he displayed is something I try to emulate with my family.

Although I might not have received the traditions handed down from him that I would have liked, it wasn't for his lack of trying. Even though he carried shame about his Indigenous heritage, he did take me out to an auntie's to pick berries, and they tanned hides, made mukluks and moccasins, and beaded. I remember those rare summers with fondness. I also had an auntie I never met send me a new pair of moccasins every year from a reserve in British Columbia. I received them until I was twelve years old but was never able to find out anything about her. That was just the family way.

After my gramps passed, I felt like a lost soul. I was devastated and took solace with my fiancé and married at age twenty. My gramps loved him, and I guess he was a good judge of character because we are still happily married. I also immersed myself in my studies and learned as much as I could about colonization and structural racism. I met my adopted *mushum* (grandfather), Clifford LaRocque, not long after, and my second male influence emerged. Clifford came into my life at a time when I was trying to reclaim my identity, and I had just met kookum Betty. He helped me to understand the self-hatred and denial in my family, and he also knew my gramps having served in the armed services as well. He took me as his granddaughter, and I learned so much about myself and my community, and I became engaged with my community. Just becoming part of the community was an incredible process. I realized that I had the privilege of serving them through the academe. My gramps set me on that path and now after so many people helping me. I could give back. I am a community-based researcher, and I serve communities. That path began when I was that little girl sitting on my gramps' lap with him whispering loving words of encouragement in my ear.

Mushum Clifford passed away eight years ago—one month after I finished the PhD he encouraged me to do. In fact, the topic was his idea, and he told me I needed to do it for the community. I was so proud to be able to hand him the manuscript because the hard copy was not yet ready. We cried tears of joy, and he whooped "Dr. Carrie Bourassa! Everyone, my granddaughter is a doctor! A Métis doctor!" This was one of the proudest moments of my life because I knew in that moment I had made both of my mushums proud.

Men have a strong influence in our lives and have important roles to play in mothering. Kookum Betty says, "our warriors will come full circle so that mothering will once again not be separated by gender."

The stories of parenting in this book speak to how lives are shaped by resistance to colonization, and how such resistance is played out in the day-to-day of parenting. Developing these narratives requires Indigenous storytelling methodology, as stories and narratives were the primary mode of transmitting knowledge in many Indigenous communities and cultures. Oral storytelling traditions remain strong among many Indigenous communities and connect us not only to our past but to our future generations. In fact, oral stories act as "intergenerational knowledge transfer" in many communities (Kovach 95). Stories that originate in and from oral traditions have personal meaning and contain traditional knowledge that is meant to be passed on to the future generations. In this book, Elder Betty McKenna shares her traditional knowledge through storytelling both in dialogue with her granddaughter, Dr. Carrie Bourassa and by writing her own chapter. Dialogue is an important way of sharing knowledge because, as Kovach notes, the relationship between story and knowing is inseparable.

Some Indigenous scholars, including Jeff Corntassell and Linda Tuhiwai Smith, argue that Indigenous storytelling is connected to our homeland and is "crucial to the cultural and political resurgence of Indigenous nations" (Corntassell 137). Corntassell argues that it is essential to rely on Indigenous storytelling considering that Indigenous history has been erased, glossed over, or retold through the lens of colonizers. He argues that there must be a "restory[ing of] the settler version of history" (138) using Indigenous storytelling:

> There is a danger in allowing colonization to be the only story of Indigenous lives. It must be recognized that colonialism is a narrative in which the Settler's power is the fundamental reference and assumption, inherently limiting Indigenous freedom and imposing a view of the world that is but an outcome or perspective on that power. (139)

Indeed, a "restorying" process is required, and we begin that process by writing this book. As Tuhiwai Smith writes,

> Storytelling, oral histories, the perspectives of elders and of women have become an integral part of all indigenous research. Each individual story is powerful. But the point about the stories is not that they simply tell a story, or tell a story simply. These new stories contribute to a collective story in which every indigenous person has a place. (145)

It is important to understand that every society's worldview is embedded in its stories—whatever kind of stories they may be. Jo-Ann Archibald, an Indigenous scholar, points out that among Indigenous peoples there are many different kinds of stories; some are sacred, historical, and cultural, whereas others are meant to relay important teachings. Other stories are owned within clans or families, and others belong to the public domain. What we share in this book are a variety of stories. Some are personal journeys, whereas others are imbued with traditional values and teachings. Everyone has a bundle and as you travel on this wheel of life, you take things into your bundle that help you on your journey. We hope that readers are able to take something that will help them on their journey for their bundle.

Opening *Listening to the Beat of Our Drums* is Elder Betty McKenna's chapter, "Research and Indigenous Research," and it cautions the reader that research is in itself ceremony and, therefore, requires careful reflection, respect, compassion, and understanding. She writes that reflective and accountable researchers must understand that their actions rearrange the lives that they come into contact with, even as researchers are themselves rearranged by these lives.

In chapter two, "Indigenous Women, Reproductive Justice, and Indigenous Feminisms: A Narrative," Darlene Juschka sets the historical context and presents three historical moments wherein colonial efforts to dominate Indigenous peoples of Canada and United States were gender focused: government conferred identity, the residential-industrial school complex, and health care. In these instances, among others, Indigenous mothering came under specific attack. Juschka argues that colonial governments, in efforts to assimilate or erase Indigeneity, targeted Indigenous gender and sexuality, and, in this effort, paid particular attention to Indigenous girls and women. The white-settler, colonial governments' foci were on Indigenous girls and women, as they are central to giving birth to the new generations.

Having set the context, Carrie Bourassa takes up the discussion of recovering Indigenous knowledge and practices in regard to mothering in chapter three, "Reclaiming Indigenous Practices in a Modern World." In this chapter, Bourassa, using Indigenous storytelling, speaks to her own life and the loss of identity and her subsequent work to find, reclaim, and share this knowledge with her daughters. Bourassa, posing a series of questions about mothering to Elder Betty McKenna in an interview, interweaves the words of Elder Betty with those of her own story of ceremony, and that of her eldest daughter Victoria.

Chapter four, "*Nîso-okâwimâwak* (Two Mothers)," engages the ideological expectations that give meaning to the concepts of mother and mothering. Both Janet Smylie and Nancy Cooper address the challenges, joys, and welcomed alliances in their journey of taking up the mantle of motherhood. This mantle carries with it expectations of heteronormativity, whiteness, and middle-class values: the Kool-Aid mom of white suburbia best evinces this trope. Facing and undercutting this trope, Smylie and Cooper tell their story of the growth of their families and becoming parents as they entered the world of in vitro fertilization.

In chapter five, "Sacred Voice Woman's Journey as an Indigenous Auntie," Paulete Poitras writes about the role of the Indigenous auntie and her coming to know the significance of this identity in her community as she took up this relationship. Reflecting on the figure of the aunt, she discusses its centrality, importance, and how the title or role is not limited to sisters but extends to other members of the larger community, who also play a role in the lives of nieces and nephews. As Paulete Poitras writes in this volume, "I was raised with the theory of 'community raising,' which says that raising a child is not just the responsibility of the parents, but it is everyone within the community."

In chapter six, "I Am a Metis Mother," Tara Turner also visits the subject of Indigenous identity, this time English Metis. Turner writes of her journey of becoming a Metis mother and how, like Bourassa, she writes of the losses accrued under colonialism but also of reclamation shared by her family of origin and her children. Her story reflects the journey she took while writing her PhD dissertation on Metis identity and in the process finding her own family narratives.

Chapter seven, "Mother Earth, Mother Mine, Mother Me, Mother Time," concludes the text and brings us full circle back to the wisdom of Elder Betty McKenna. In this last chapter, Elder Betty reflects on Indigenous mothering and her own experiences with her mother, family, and community. Taking us back in time, she speaks of her own childhood and how she learned through ceremony and teachings the sacred path of mothering. With this in mind Elder Betty might say, "One is not born a mother, one becomes a mother."

WORKS CITED

Archibald, JoAnn. *Indigenous Storywork: Educating the Heart, Mind, Body, and Spirit.* University of British Columbia Press, Print.

Corntassell, Jeff. "Indigenous Storytelling, Truth-telling, and Community Approaches to Reconciliation." *English Studies in Canada*, vol. 35, no. 1, 2009, pp. 137-159. *Research Gate*, doi: 10.1353/esc.0.0163

Kovach, Margaret. *Indigenous Methodologies: Characteristics,*

Conversations, and Contexts. University of Toronto Press, 2009.
Tuhiwai Smith, Linda. *Decolonizing Methodologies: Research and Indigenous Peoples*. ZED Books, 2012.

1.
Research and Indigenous Research

ELDER BETTY MCKENNA

I WOULD LIKE TO OPEN this book by talking a bit about research and Indigenous research. We say that ceremony is research, but research is also ceremony, so before students take it upon themselves to do any type of research with our people in our communities, I'd like them to think about this statement: if we talk about ceremony, and we're talking about research being ceremony, then prepare for a ceremony. Equally, there are protocols, and there are ethical constructs around ceremony. In light of this, one needs to prepare for research, just as one prepares for ceremony. Such preparation entails researchers finding within them their unique physical, spiritual, mental, and emotional balance. There are no two researchers alike who will find the same thing because we are individuals brought into this world by the Creator. Our body comes from Mother Earth and when creator and earth come together in our bodies, there is a rearrangement, so to speak, of life. Before anyone was born the sun shone and the wind blew and it was a beautiful world. Then after someone is born the sun shines, the wind blows and it's a beautiful world, but when that person is born into this world there's a rearrangement. Equally so with researchers, and, therefore, they must look at themselves as they prepare for research. There needs to be a rearrangement of the physical, mental, emotional, and spiritual as they develop their research. Researchers rearrange themselves from the inside out and look at their life and community, education, and where they are located in that whole schema of family, education, and community.

Before a researcher goes into Indigenous communities, they need to know that they will never be exactly like any one of the people in our communities, since each individual in these communities came into this world and rearranged everything about the cosmos just like we all did. And when we leave, when our body goes back to Mother Earth and our spirit goes back to the Great Spirit life is rearranged again. So we go into those communities with a rearranged idea and thought patterns and feelings about our research.

One thing I want researchers to remember is not to take ownership of the story and instead take the position of "this is my viewpoint" and "this is someone else's viewpoint." If perhaps a researcher goes into a community, and their method of research is through talking circles and with people sharing their ideas and their thoughts, the researcher should think of it as people having different plates of food. You go in and there is fruit, there is meat, there are vegetables, so the person with a bowl of blueberries presents their blueberries, their life story, to the researcher. Then the person who has raspberries presents their life story—their way of thinking, and worldview. Their life story is about raspberries, so they're not the same even if they come from the same community. Their ideas are different and the flavour of their understanding is different even if on the surface Indigenous peoples may look and speak the same. This similarity does not mean to say we are the same. It is not a case of everyone needing to agree; rather it is a case of listening and being able to understand—from one's standpoint—what is being said, and sometimes what is being said will not be understood for maybe ten to fifteen years.

It is helpful for researchers to think of their work as preparing for ceremony. When I prepare for ceremony, I look at the protocols we need to do, and we need to make sure we are taking care of ourselves mentally, which can be done by mental preparation. One thinks about all the things that need to be done mentally. Also, one needs to think of things that need to be done physically, such as getting enough sleep. Furthermore, before ceremony begins, one needs to go out and put down offerings. Traditionally, I had always been told we put down tobacco before we go to ceremony, and when we do this, we say to the Creator, "I'm going to a ceremony, see me here and I'm doing something for myself, for my whole life and body, for my mind and my spirit." For many Indigenous people, mind and body and spirit are not separated. When we come into this world, we have a spirit and we have a body. I often ask people what they think is more important your body or your spirit? My answer is neither one is more important than the other because they're never separated, and they never were. Before we're born, we were our spirit, and our body was a part of Mother Earth, and our spirit was a part of the Great Mystery, the *gitchimado*, and even Mother Earth is a part of *gitchimado*. The *gitchimado* rearranges everything when we are brought into this world. And when we pass away, our body is rearranged; it goes back to Mother Earth, and our spirit goes back to *gitchimado*, and it is just the same as before we were born. Recall what I said, "before we are born, the sun shines, the wind blows, and it is a beautiful world, and after we are born, the sun still shines, the wind still blows, and it is a beautiful world; nothing changes."

Why do we call that sun, Grandfather Sun? There is a reason we say Grandfather Sun: because a wealthy man and a poor man can sit out on the grass and that sun will shine on both their faces. It is no different for the poor man than it is for the wealthy man. It is the same for Grandmother Moon: she is in that sky shining just as brightly for a poor woman as she does a wealthy woman. We say the sun and moon are our grandfather and grandmother, as we learn from them just as we learn from our grandmothers and grandfathers. They put the learning that they have into stories they tell us: a story is a story, a person's life is a person's life, and together they provide something new.

If we value Indigenous research, and we want to work with Indigenous communities, then we need to look at those communities as a very diverse, wonderful circle—a sacred circle. If we call our research sacred, then we are talking about sacred beings sharing their lives. What is more sacred than their feelings and ideas? And no one owns them—no researcher can own that which is grown from that community. If it grows from that community it should be harvested by that community. True growth and order and adequacy, love, security, social approval, and self-esteem go back to the ceremony at the beginning of life, and everyone had a beginning of life.

Migwitch

2.
Indigenous Women, Reproductive Justice, and Indigenous Feminisms

A Narrative

DARLENE JUSCHKA

PREAMBLE

AS A WHITE SETTLER and a poststructural feminist living and working on the prairie, I have come to know myself differently. I did not always live on the prairie but came to the skies and the wind later in my life. On the prairie you get to know both very well. It was on the prairie that I was more fully introduced to, and schooled in, Indigenous critical theory and Indigenous feminisms, and for this, I am grateful and ever mindful that the knowledge I was gifted with is not mine to keep; it is to be shared. In this chapter, then, I share what I have learned and put it into my own forms of expression, leaving me, and not my teachers, accountable for my story.

INTRODUCTION

The Indigenous peoples of Turtle Island (named North America—that is Canada, United States, and Mexico—by colonizers) have endured long years of colonization, which has taken multiple forms, but in all, its manifestations were intent on removing Indigenous peoples from Turtle Island. White settler governments were formed, nations were built, and Indigenous peoples were colonized. And although treaties were made between some Indigenous groups and white settler governments, the latter have not been faithful to their promises. Indeed, their every letter, note, policy, and act was oriented toward the erasure of Indigeneity. Some of these efforts took the form of defining "Indian" identity, education, and healthcare. These efforts were resisted by Indigenous peoples over the hundreds of years of colonization, and with that, Indigenous identities have survived.

This chapter examines how colonial governments in Canada and the United States sought to erase Indigeneity. In particular, I pay attention to efforts that focused on Indigenous girls and women because they have always been central to giving birth to the new generations—knowledge of which white settler governments were cognizant. To consider the erasure of Indigeneity through girls and women, I look at three manifestations of colonial dominance: government conferred identity, the residential and industrial school complexes, and healthcare; all instances of which gender came into play, and Indigenous mothering came under specific attack. By denying Indigenous women the capacity to confer Indigenous identity, by traumatizing Indigenous girls, by manipulating Indigenous girls' and women's bodies, and by abducting children from Indigenous mothers, the colonial states of Canada and United States attempted to wipe out Indigenous communities. Such attempts did not go unchallenged, and the final sections of this chapter discuss resilience and forms of resistance along with the critical engagement of colonialism by Indigenous feminisms.

COLONIZATION, GENDER IDEOLOGY, AND INDIGENOUS IDENTITY

The gender orthodoxies of Indigenous sociocultural formations of North America that Eurowestern colonists encountered often reflected what is called "gender equivalency": that is, an integrated set of practices, attitudes, and beliefs with regard to gender wherein all genders, though variant, are seen to be equivalent in value (Juschka). These gender equivalent relations were based on social roles, cultural and spiritual knowledge, relations with the environment, and affiliations with the spiritual (Roscoe). Equally, different genders had particular expertise related to specific areas of knowledge, such as healing, herb lore, foodstuffs, stories, sings, rites, planting, time, science and technology, and so forth

(Juschka). The equivalency of gender operated in tandem with a worldview of interrelatedness, wherein all life and nonlife were connected and, therefore, shared in importance. Knowledge—be it ritual, ecological, spiritual, technological, historical, sociological, political and so forth—was deemed significant regardless of who held it (Juschka).[1]

However, with contact, colonization, and white settler occupation of Turtle Island, Indigenous peoples were located as the "other," and a significant aspect of the othering was formulated by recourse to (idealized) European gender ideologies that were represented as normative and were subsequently imposed on Indigenous peoples.[2] Sheila McManus wrote of the colonization of the Blackfoot peoples (Siksika/Blackfoot, Pikuni/Peigan, Kainah/Blood) in western Turtle Island:

> Containing the Blackfoot on small patches of land with herds of cattle and European-style dwellings was only one set of goals Canadian and American officials shared when it came to reshaping the Blackfeet into a more acceptable (or at least invisible) piece of the nation. They also wanted to alter the gender norms of adults at a more fundamental level. Officials wanted to end polygamous marriages; make aboriginal women behave like submissive, domesticated Euro-North American women; and make aboriginal men behave like farmers, all of which involved imposing their own ideas of appropriate femininity and masculinity. (97)

By the mid-1800s, settlement was the dominant form of colonization, as evidenced by the *U.S. Homestead Act* of 1862 and the *Canadian Dominion Lands Act* of 1871. Both Acts meant the appropriation of Indigenous lands, but also included was a process of "domestication" and/or annihilation of the Indigenous peoples of Turtle Island. Domestication took the form of the imposition of European gender ideologies on Indigenous peoples. For colonization to be successful, it was necessary to dismantle the gender fluidity and equivalent gender relations among Indigenous peoples: divide and conquer has always been a frequently practised hegemonic strategy (Juschka).

The play of power, however, is a two-way street, and although the colonizer had the majority of power, contact with Indigenous peoples in the late 1800s, particularly Indigenous women, may well have laid the groundwork for early feminism. Seneca (Iroquois) women were present at the Seneca Falls Convention held in New York in 1848 and supported white settler women's bid for the vote. The feminist Lucretia Mott, with other like-minded Quaker women's rights activists at the conference, drew on her discussions with Seneca women to shape her contribution toward a definition of women's rights (Hewitt 37).

During the early centuries of colonization, Indigenous women of Turtle Island often acted as liaisons between Indigenous and white settler governing bodies and were authoritative in both groups (Shoemaker). Nanye-hi (Nancy Ward), for example, sought to find peace between the Cherokee and white settlers. Ward has been named the "Beloved Woman" by the Cherokee because of her bravery in battle. As the Beloved Woman, she had say over the lives of prisoners of war and participated in negotiations between Cherokee and white settlers. However, over time and under pressure from white settler and masculinist governments, Cherokee social organization shifted toward a more patriarchal model, and Nanye-hi was the last woman to be named the Beloved Woman (Perdue, *Cherokee Women*).

Over time, and in connection with the second wave of colonization and with the arrival of white settler women, the status of Indigenous women became increasingly precarious in white settler societies. Missionaries and white women spoke avidly against liaisons between Indigenous women and white fur traders; moreover, British and French law did not recognize these marriages, allowing or forcing men to return to Europe and leave behind their Indigenous wives, children, relatives, and friends (McManus 98). In the middle and later period of settlement and appropriation of land (the seventeenth until eighteenth century), the marriage of primarily male settlers with Indigenous women was tolerated but frowned upon. By the late-nineteenth and early-twentieth century, however, it was made illegal throughout the United States with miscegenation laws (Stubblefield). With the imposition of white settler gender ideologies and the coming of missionaries and white settler women, the status of Indigenous women as viable, powerful, and informed members of Indigenous societies began a downward spiral. In the social stratification of the new colonies, Indigenous women were placed at the bottom and were oppressed by white men, white women, and, subsequently, Indigenous men.

Prior to the *Indian Act* of 1876, there had been a gradual shift toward tightening up and regulating all things related to the Indigenous peoples of Canada. For example, in an Act for the Better Protection of the Lands and Property of the Indians in Lower Canada, passed in 1850 and referring to occupation of reserve lands, the definition of Indigenous included "all those of Indian blood and their descendants, non-Indians who have married Indians living on the designated lands, and even persons adopted in infancy by Indians" (Canada, *Report of the Royal Commission* 24). Within a year, this legislation became more restrictive and denied non-Indigenous men who married Indigenous women the right to claim status, but status could be acquired by non-Indigenous woman who married Indigenous men. The descendants of these intermarriages who resided on reserve land would be thought of as Indigenous, regardless of the status of the female spouse. It was at this juncture that Indigenous status is developed within patrilineal systems of identity and inheritance.

The concept of enfranchisement was introduced in 1857 through an act that continued to encourage the gradual "civilization," as white settlers deemed it, of Indigenous peoples in Canada. The act applied to both Upper and Lower Canada and gave voting rights to Indigenous adult men who, if they sought enfranchisement, lost their Indigenous status. Instead, they would operate within white settler society, although they would still receive land and a sum of money equal to that of members of the band, and they could continue to live on reserve land. The spouse and children of an enfranchised Indigenous adult man were also enfranchised when he was, and they also lost their Indigenous status. Equally though, neither could vote, and the enfranchised Indigenous woman did not receive a share of reserve land, as at this time, the effort was to ensure Indigenous women were properly submissive to their husbands (McManus). If the man died, for example, and if there were no children, she could inherit his estate and live on the land until her death, whereupon ownership of the land would revert to the Crown. This approach is part of the Gradual Civilization Act of 1857, wherein white settler governments became the legal body that determined Indigenous status and who was or was not Indigenous (Canada, *Report of the Royal Commission* 24).

In the Gradual Enfranchisement Act of 1869, Indigenous women continued to lose their rights. Operating within white settler masculine hegemony, Indigenous women were explicitly denied the right to vote in band elections, since voting was restricted to adult men only, as it was in white settler society. Further, drawing from the *Gradual Civilization Act*, an Indigenous woman who married an Indigenous man from another band lost membership in her home band, as did her children, becoming members of the husband's band. No similar provisions applied to Indigenous men who married non-Indigenous women, nor did they lose treaty payments. In these two acts covering the period between 1850 and 1869, Indigenous women lost social, political, and economic power and status, and faced the intersection of colonial, racial, and sexual discrimination in Canada. They essentially lost the right to produce Indigenous children; only Indigenous men could do that.

The *Indian Act* of 1876 instituted Indigenous women's status as subordinate to that of Indigenous men.[3] The method of tracing descent through the male, or the patrilineal line, was imposed on Indigenous peoples of Canada. The Iroquois confederacy of the Great Lakes region of Canada, the Tlingit, Haida, and Tsimshian of British Columbia, for example, all traced descent through the mother's line (matrilineal), as clan mothers were powerful women. With colonization identity and status were confirmed on men of the group through patrilineal relations, and Indigenous women lost their status as well as social and political power (Green, "Canaries in the Mines of Citizenship" 723; Bourassa et al. 296-97).

In 1951, the Indian Act was revised again, and a number of new provisions again negatively affected the lives of Indigenous women. The Act used the language of blood to identify and establish Indigenous status. In this amendment, the language of registration was also used in order to confer Indigenous status. Those registered as Indians would be the only persons to be recognized as Indian and, therefore, the only ones able to occupy reserve land and to receive treaty annuity payments and band money distribution. Many who had been involuntarily enfranchised—mistakenly struck from band membership or simply overlooked—would not qualify for status under this amendment. They had to be registered with the band to secure Indian status (Green, "Canaries" 723).

Secondly, with this amendment the double mother rule was applied. In this ruling, a child lost status at age twenty-one if their mother and grandmother had obtained status only through marriage to a man with Indigenous status. This ruling had further ramifications for Indigenous women and their children. If Indigenous women lost status under Canadian law so did their children and grandchildren: identity was again conferred through the paternal line and not the maternal one. The masculine hegemonic blinders of the government caused immense grief to Indigenous peoples of both genders (Bourassa et al.; Canada, *Report of the Royal Commission*; Green, "Canaries in the Mines of Citizenship"; Green, "Balancing Strategies").

Between 1951 and 1985, during the emergence of mid-twentieth-century feminisms, there was a growing awareness of inequality and the lack of civil rights by the general population in many Eurowestern countries. By the 1960s, the African-American civil rights movement, the American Indian movement, the antiwar movement, the women's movement, and the push for global decolonization all challenged oppressive social structures. They fought the racism, sexism, and colonialism inherent to the legal, political, educational, and religious institutions of Canada and United States. However, as Carrie Bourassa and her colleagues argue, "In the end, the amendments secured by Indigenous peoples did not repair the damage or previous legislation. Kinship ties, cultural ties, and participation in governance were significantly disrupted. Long terms consequences for these women and their children would include the erosion of connections and rights" (298).

INDUSTRIAL AND RESIDENTIAL SCHOOLS: "NEVER ENOUGH TO EAT"

Indigenous mothering was directly challenged by the introduction of residential schools in Canada and industrial schools in the United

States. In the late-nineteenth and early-twentieth century, boarding schools became the norm rather than schools on the reserves in Canada and the United States. One significant effort of these Christian-run schools was "to take the Indian out of the girl or boy." The history of these schools, and their abuse of Indigenous children, has become part of mainstream knowledge in Canada, particularly in light of the Truth and Reconciliation Commission. For over one hundred years, residential and industrial schools operated as both a necessary and productive way to assist in the "civilization" of Indigenous children. This kind of thinking continued to dominant the views of the government, even though it had become apparent Indigenous children were abused, some to death. Parents' resistance to their children being taken was often met with starvation or imprisonment enacted by the government officials on behalf of residential schools.

Working with Christian institutional authorities, the Canadian and United States federal governments determined that the best way to assimilate, and therefore erase, Indigenous peoples was through their children. Education, like healthcare, was a treaty right, but rather than governments providing education, they instead set up mechanisms intent on "kill[ing] the Indian in order to save the man" (qtd. in Engel et al. 281). There had initially been on-reserve and/or local schools, but boarding schools became the preferred choice for governments intent on assimilation. Christian institutions, intent on conversions, agreed to develop these boarding schools. Indeed, there had been a general agreement between Anglicans and Catholics in some locations of Canada as to who had jurisdictional oversight of Indigenous peoples (Williams 3-4). Whether Anglican, Catholic, Methodist, Presbyterian, or United Church, these religious institutions worked with governments to produce an extensive systemic structure for the eradication of Indigenous peoples of Turtle Island. The Truth and Reconciliation Commission of Canada and the 2008 Boarding School Healing Project of United States have exposed the horrendous abuse and exploitation in these schools. In Canada, off-reserve residential schools began in 1879. In the 1920s and early 1930s, they were thriving. In 1969, Indian Affairs took control of the schools, but by 1986, most schools had closed or were turned over to bands.

In 1996, the last school, located in Punnichy, Saskatchewan, was closed (*Honouring the Truth* 3). Over their existence, the schools housed approximately one third of the Indigenous peoples of Canada (Engel et al. 280). In the United States, off-reserve industrial schools began about the same time as in Canada with the founding of the Carlisle Indian School in Pennsylvania in 1879. The school was founded by Captain Richard Pratt, the military man who authored the phrase "Kill the Indian in order to save the man." Residential and industrial schools were harsh environments and took the lives of many Indigenous children. According to the Truth and Reconciliation Commission of Canada, the death rate for children in residential schools was almost five times higher than the general death rate of non-residential school children (*Honouring the Truth* 93), and although they did not record the deaths of students, boarding schools in the United States were, nonetheless, sites for the transmission of communicable diseases, such as tuberculosis (Adam 132-133). Madeline Engel and her colleagues write:

> In Canada, the schools were overcrowded, students were malnourished and, according to government records, communicable diseases, especially tuberculosis, resulted in death rates of 40 percent to almost 70 percent in one decade.... Even in the early 1900s an overall death rate of 24 percent characterized the boarding school population. (238)

Having separated Indigenous children from their parents, these schools further prevented siblings from interacting with one another in order to ensure that the children would leave behind their Indigenous ways of being. Indigenous posture, hair, mannerisms, languages, dress, interactions, games, and knowledge were emphatically suppressed in order to emplace a not-quite-citizen who would work cheaply and efficiently for proper citizens—that is, white settlers. Typically, Indigenous girls were taught domestic work and Indigenous boys about manual labour (Smith, *Indigenous Peoples and Boarding Schools*). Vibrant and essential Indigenous knowledge was represented as backward and pagan (Williams), and severely repressed in the schools. Interaction between Indigenous children was heavily monitored, while they were taught to quash their empathy for one another. Irma Bos, a student at Alberni Residential School, for example, remembers it as "a sad place to have gone, cause kids used to cry, cry at night ... sometimes another girl would get into bed with whoever was crying just to, to comfort them. And ahh, the supervisor used to come in and ... they'd [the comforters] get strapped or hit" (qtd. in de Leeuw, "Intimate Colonialisms" 353). Kindness, gentleness, concern, curiosity, even humour—all qualities of good parenting—were disciplined from the children. Another student, Victoria McIntosh learned never to trust anyone: "You learn not to cry anymore. You just get harder. And yeah, you learn to shut down" (qtd. in *Honouring the Truth* 42-43).

Family separation, sibling separation, and gender separation were mechanisms by which the white settler residential and industrial school systems sought to control Indigenous peoples of Turtle Island. So harsh were the conditions over the 150 years of the operation of residential and industrial schools that many Indigenous children took their own lives. Death was better than the boarding school. The separate sphere gender ideology of the early twentieth century divided the male and female: the male was prepared for the public sphere, and the female for the domestic sphere. In this model of family formation, the patriarch ruled the family with the support and obedience from the wife and mother. This structure, of course, was an ideal promoted by white settler men, whose own lives did not often reflect this kind of gender reality insofar as their wives often had more power than not. Gender organization among Indigenous peoples of Canada and the United States varied but tended to operate in a balanced fashion so that females, males, and other genders had status within the social body and made decisions and contributions to it. Women could and did make decisions and moved about freely within their communities (Henning). Such movement, however, was perceived as highly problematic. The Canadian state was perplexed by the autonomy and freedom of movement of Indigenous women and disapprovingly called it "promiscuity" (McManus 99). The separate spheres gender ideologies of the French and English, and Christian white settlers were treated as normative and necessary for Indigenous peoples to adopt if they were to become properly "civilized" (Juschka). Hierarchy and power-over relations were normative to most Eurowestern social systems and, therefore, seen a normative to proper human evolution (Carter; de Leeuw, "Intimate Colonialisms"; and Smith, *Indigenous Peoples and Boarding Schools*).

Starvation and inedible food were part of the lives of Indigenous children in residential schools in Canada and the U.S. Parents of children frequently complained of their children's physical condition as they were "underfed and severely malnourished" (Mosby 149). John Milloy, quoting Reverend A. Lett, writes how "many children at too many schools ... lived out their lives ... 'ill-fed and ill-clothed and turned out into the cold to work'; they were trapped, 'unhappy with a feeling of slavery existing in their minds, no aims, no feelings' and no way to escape except in 'thought'—in their imagination and memories of home" (110). Children endured starvation rations and malnourishment, which led to illnesses, such as the flu or tuberculosis (Mosby 149). The condition of the schools themselves was also a travesty. Most had been badly located with little shelter and had been poorly constructed. Over time, they began to crumble (Milloy; Canada, *Report of the Royal Commission*; de Leeuw, "Intimate Colonialisms"; Smith, *Indigenous Peoples and Boarding Schools*).

Abuses were also common in residential schools and took every imagined form. Coercion and violence were common place as children were punished for infractions determined by the staff of the schools. The government did not institute regulations concerning physical punishment of the children until 1937, whereupon a circular had been sent out speaking to proper procedures (Milloy 140). It did little, however, to prevent the abuse and neglect of Indigenous children in the schools. John Milloy's study of residential schools in Canada catalogues the abuses and notes that many children attempted to flee the punishment but died in the process—as seen in the tragedy of eight-year-old Duncan Sticks who, in 1902, froze to death fleeing physical punishment by staff at Williams Lake Industrial School in British Columbia. Four young boys in 1937 fled from brutality, this time from the Lejac Residential School, British Columbia, only to freeze to death as well (Milloy 142-43). The children were found in light clothing, one without shoes.

Children also suffered sexual abuse at the schools. Staff, religious and lay, preyed on the children, as did older students, who themselves had been abused by staff when younger. Jean Oakes, an elder of the Nekaneet people of Saskatchewan, once commented to Candace Savage that "these nuns and priests, they use to treat girls bad" (Savage 165). Sarah de Leeuw wrote that "Aboriginal girls and young women were particularly susceptible to the bodily implication of colonialism.... It should perhaps come as no little surprise that the testimonies of former residential school students include (albeit very scant) recollections of pregnancy and abortion within the schools" ("Intimate Colonialisms" 349-350). With the sterilization acts in British Columbia and Alberta, school officials could also sterilize any Indigenous children under their charge, another mechanism for dealing with the undesired reproduction of Indigenous peoples. Sterilization of groups of children could occur once they reached puberty (Pegoraro 162).

Indigenous parents frequently resisted sending their children to residential schools, but the Canadian and United States governments had made it illegal for Indigenous parents not to send their children to residential or industrial schools. The primary intention of the schools was assimilation, not education, which was why governments ensured children went. One mechanism to force Indigenous peoples to send their children to boarding schools was the withholding of rations until children were given over (Williams 201; Adams 211). In one instance, an older woman, whose rations had been withheld, finally turned her children over to Qu'Appelle Industrial School in Saskatchewan, only to die several days later from starvation and tuberculosis (Williams 202). By 1920, Indigenous parents who did not surrender their children faced criminal charges (de Leeuw, "If Anything" 130), whereas children who refused to go could be charged with truancy and sent to a reformatory school, a place possibly more violent than the boarding schools (Pisciotta). Indigenous parents resisted governments, but in the face of starvation and jail, and with their children threatened with reform schools, they reluctantly acquiesced. The actions of governments and associated Christian institutions disrupted Indigenous parenting, which was a way to "kill the Indian." As Mary-Ellen Kelm argues:

> A major function of the residential schools, according to Frank Pedley, deputy superintendent of Indian Affairs in 1902, was the removal of pupils from the retrogressive influence of home life. Central to this view was the notion that Aboriginal parents were negligent parents and especially that unassimilated Native women made poor mothers. ("A Scandalous Procession" 55)

When residential schools began to close their doors in the 1960s—the federal government officially closed them in Canada in 1996, but in the United States, most were not closed until 2007—the next government intervention Indigenous parents faced was called the "Sixties Scoop," which actually lasted until the late 1980s in Canada (Engel et al. 287; *Honouring the Truth* 68-69). The Sixties Scoop was the removal of Indigenous children from their homes for adoption, and it reflected the continuing belief of white settler governments that Indigenous parents, particularly mothers, were unfit. This determination of unfitness was measured in part by the degree of assimilation into Eurowestern social organizations, and in particular by the assimilation of white settler gender ideology of the subordination and domesticity of the female and feminine to the dominating male and masculine (Smith, *Conquest* 37).

In Canada, the Sixties Scoop was based on colonialist, racist, and misguided views about Indigenous peoples of Canada. Indigenous mothers, fathers, and families had children removed for reasons such as poverty, a situation imposed on them by the same government removing their children. Indigenous culture and language continued to be viewed as problematic, as was Indigenous women's autonomy, particularly sexual autonomy, and as a result, many infants and toddlers were taken away from their mothers. The summary of Truth and Reconciliation states that " in 1977, Aboriginal children accounted for 44% of the children in care in Alberta, 51% of the children in care in Saskatchewan, and 60% of the children in care in Manitoba" (*Honouring the Truth* 69). Moreover, from the 1960s through the 1980s, eleven thousand

Indigenous children in Canada were taken from their homes by provincial social workers (Engel et al. 288). Although this problem was made apparent and steps were taken to prevent adoptions of Indigenous children in the 1980s, Indigenous children continue to be removed from their homes through foster care (Engel et al 289).

In the United States, orphanages for Indigenous children developed as a result of the wide-scale death of Indigenous peoples, particular parents. As in Canada, the industrial school system was a place where Indigenous children were placed should their parents die. Extended family relations were never considered, since such relations were seen as "uncivilized" in the view of white settler ideology. In 1958, the Indian Adoption Project was established, and it operated until 1967. Over this period, seven hundred Indigenous children were placed in non-Indigenous homes, and although adoption ceased, removal and foster care have not: "In South Dakota, Native American children constituted 7 percent of the population, but comprised 54 percent of children placed in adoptive homes by the Department of Public Welfare; and in Wisconsin, Indian children were separated from their parents at a rate 1,600 times than that of non-Indian children" (Engel et al. 290).

INDIGENOUS GIRLS AND WOMEN, AND STERILIZATION

Even if some nineteenth-century white settler feminists learned from and worked with Indigenous women, what would become mainstream white-settler feminism was shaped by the knowledge systems of the time and was, therefore, infused with the narrative of colonialism, which combined Indigeneity, racism, heteronormativity, and Christianity to produce the figure of the colonized Indigenous subject who was in need of civilizing. And if that failed, then the Indigenous "other" would be allowed to "die off"; although this so-called dying off typically took the form of murder enacted through warfare, slaughter, starvation, and contracted illnesses. The American Secretary of the Interior Henry Teller wrote in 1883 that "contact has come between the settler and the Indian in all parts of the country. Civilization and savagery cannot dwell together ... [the Indigenous person] must adopt the 'white man's ways' or be swept away by the vices of savage life" (qtd. in McManus 63).

Mixed with early twentieth century Social Darwinism, the Eugenics movement of the late nineteenth and twentieth centuries proposed the necessity to cleanse and purify the social body in order that human evolution arrive at its proper end in history. During this period, sociology, medicine, biology, legal studies and other sites for the production of knowledge such as Christian institutions in Canada assumed that there were racial distinctions between people. This way of thinking was actively engaged, for example, by the "famous five" who were central to passing the 1928 *Sterilization Act* in Alberta (Moss, Stam and Kattevilder). Nellie McClung along with Emily Murphy, Henrietta Muir Edwards, Louise McKinney, and Irene Parlby were eugenicists who held to the view of the necessity to purify of the human species in order that it might achieve proper human evolution (Moss, Stam and Kattevilder 109; Stote 144-45, n.19). The "famous five" may have secured personhood for women, but those women were white, middle-class to elite and largely Christian. They were also opposed the immigration into Canada of those classified as non-whites.

Eugenics, enacted by the medical establishment in Canada, involved, in one form, the sterilization of peoples considered to be drains on the nation and its resources. The so-called feeble-minded (closely linked to the feminine, since the female was seen as intellectually incapable) and the figures of the criminal, the insane, the moron, and the destitute were all applied to Indigenous peoples of North America (Stote 125). American and Canadian governments could then deny any active efforts on their part to reduce Indigenous populations by using the above categories to justify why Indigenous women (and men to a lesser degree) were legally sterilized well into the 1970s in Canada.

The sterilization of the Indigenous women of Turtle Island was practiced in both Canada and the United States from the outset of colonization in one form or another. Colonization, in both locations, was a process of elimination and assimilation. Such practices, many felt, would ensure the demise of Indigenous peoples, and it was not until the 1900s with concrete evidence of an increase in Indigenous populations that other means of control, such as medical sterilization, were brought into play (Ralstin-Lewis 77). Leonardo Pegoraro writes that "The 'surgical' solution or 'eugenicide' ... began its legal history when J. Frank Hanly, Governor of Indiana, on 9 April 1907 signed a law authorizing the compulsory sterilization of any criminal, idiot, rapist, or mentally demented" (163). Each of these socially constructed categories was loosely defined and applied in order to target certain demographic groups in Canada and the United States. Anna Stubblefield writes the following:

> J. Langdon Down, whose name is still invoked in the classification of "Down Syndrome," based his understanding of intellectual deficiency on theories like Chambers'. Expounding upon his original 1866 publication, "Ethnic Classification of Idiots," Down wrote, "I was struck by the remarkable resemblance of feeble-minded children to the various ethnic types of the human family." He proceeded to discuss white feebleminded children who, "from some deteriorating influence" had been "removed into another ethnic type" and therefore resembled so-called Negro, Malay, North American Indian, or Mongolian people. (171)

Indigenous peoples were marked as uncivilized and impure, and were perceived to be a general threat to white settler social formations. And in response to this purported threat, Indigenous women's bodies were surveilled (Stubblefield 178-179). Certainly, Indigenous boys and men also faced surveillance, and at times reproductive oppression, but their surveillance tended to be focused more on the mind than the body, although the body was certainly used as a vehicle to control the mind. This odd approach reflects Eurowestern gender ideologies, wherein the female and feminine are associated with the body and the male and masculine with the mind. Lewis Terman, a Stanford psychologist, was a leading expert in developing intelligence tests and a supporter of eugenics. He wrote the following in his 1916 text *The Measure of Intelligence*:

> Their [children] dullness seems to be racial, or at least inherent in the family stocks from which they come. The fact that one meets this type with such extraordinary frequency among Indians, Mexicans, and negroes [sic] suggests quite forcibly that the whole question of racial differences in men-

> tal traits will have to be taken up anew and by experimental methods.... Children of this group should be segregated in special classes and be given instruction which is concrete and practical. They cannot master abstractions, but they often can be made efficient workers, able to look out for themselves. There is no possibility at present of convincing society that they should not be allowed to reproduce, although from a eugenic point of view they constitute a grave problem because of their unusually prolific breeding. (qtd. in Chávez-García 217-218)

Anna Stubblefield writes that in the area of family studies, feeblemindedness was linked to morality and, subsequently, became the means to "deal with" the moral problems of "pauperism, sexual promiscuity, criminality, and vagabondage" (125). From the 1920s until the 1950s, eugenics flourished in Eurowestern knowledge systems and shaped medicine, the law, the government, and opinions of the general population, who were repeatedly told by respected authorities that Indigenous peoples, and all peoples marked by race, were deficient (Stubblefield 163).

In Canada, the provinces of Alberta and British Columbia both established a sexual sterilization act that was operative between 1928 and 1972, and 1933 and 1973, respectively. Other provinces in Canada did not have an explicit sterilization act but equally engaged in the practice of coercive sterilization within the framework of eugenics. As in the United States, the process was one of declaring the individual incompetent, and if of reproductive age, then measures were taken to ensure the individual did not (further) reproduce. In 1937, in order to ensure that governments were not implicated in racial genocide, the act was amended so that consent prior to sterilization was necessary; consent from those deemed "mentally defective," however, was not necessary. Karen Stote has written that "the proportion of Aboriginal peoples sterilized by the Act rose steadily from 1939 onward, tripling from 1949-1959.... Consent for sterilization was only sought in 17 percent of Aboriginal cases. More than 77 percent were defined as mentally defective and hence their consent was not needed" (120-121).

The criteria of mental defectiveness were broad and included judgments with regard to morality. In the frame of eugenics and then later "population control" (popular from the 1950s to the 1980s), sexual activity outside of the boundary of marriage, promiscuity, and an unwillingness to be subordinate to white settlers, particularly men, were all criteria that signified the individual to be mentally defective (Stote). Doctors' letters used in trial transcripts draw on the trope of sexual promiscuous Indian women to legitimate their sterilization. Seen in physician records, waywardness and promiscuity were primary criteria for the sterilization of women in general and Indigenous women in particular. The supervisor of social services wrote a summary to the Eugenics Board concerning an Indigenous woman in his care:

> The patient is a mental defective, with numerous behaviour problems, particularly being promiscuous and associating with undesirables. Sterilization is, therefore, strongly recommended to prevent patient from having illegitimate children which the community would have to care for and for whom it would be very difficult to find foster homes. (qtd. in Stote 122)

Improper sexual behaviour, including same-sex relations, could locate one if racialized or Indigenous in the "medical industrial complex," as Barbara Gurr names it (35).

Sterilizations did not stop when the doctrine of eugenics decreased in popularity. Population control, shaped in line as it was with Thomas Malthus's essay "On the Principal of Population" (1798), carried forward its concerns with regard to increased population, paired with a view of sex as a threat to human existence. His essay provides the basis for the theory and practice of population control in the United States conducted through such methods as the sterilization of Indigenous peoples as a so-called undesirable population: undesirable in large part because they stood in the way of access to minerals on reserve lands, and to whom the government owed resources as part of treaty agreements. And, once again although both Indigenous males and females were targeted, reproductive Indigenous girls and women were the primary targets.

In the United States, the Indian Health Services (IHS) became a primary site for the sterilization of Indigenous women. Work done by the group Women of All Red Nations, by Indigenous feminist Wilma Mankiller, and by academics Myla Vincenti Carpio, Jane Lawrence, Andrea Smith, and Karen Stote, among others, have shown that Indigenous women had a higher incident of sterilization than white settler women. Moreover, many of these surgeries were done without the knowledge or consent of the woman, or the women were coerced into the operation. It has been estimated that 42 percent of reproductive Indigenous women of the United States were sterilized between 1968 and 1982 (Gurr 125). Enough Indigenous women were sterilized in the United States that Myla Vincenti Caprio has lamented for a lost generation. Marie Ralstin-Lewis discusses the impact of sterilization:

> From 1970 to 1980, the birthrate for Indian women fell at a rate seven times greater than that of white women. This dramatic statistic indicates that the sterilization and birth control campaign was significantly more than an attack on women in general: it was a systematic program aimed at reducing the Native population, or genocide. (72)

Caprio has argued that the eugenics prior to World War II was translated into population control and although the discourse shifted over time, the outcomes did not (40). Andrea Smith, among other Indigenous scholars of the United States, has argued that the sterilization of Indigenous women was a direct effort of the United States government to deal with the so-called Indian problem. Sterilization was promoted to Indigenous women (and women of colour in general in the United States) as a method of birth control during the 1960s and 1970s. Other Indigenous women were sterilized without their knowledge, sterilized just after a birth, or were sterilized as a measure to deal with another issue (Smith, "Not an Indian Tradition" 80-83).

Reproductive healthcare in the United States for Indigenous women, and women of colour, has been and continues to be problematic. Limited healthcare combined with limited resources embedded in a neocolonial context of the United States has meant that healthcare for Indigenous peoples, rooted in eugenics and population control, has not been in their best interests. Instead, healthcare was the means by which to control, experiment, and reduce the number of Indigenous peoples. Drawing on a study of IHS physicians performing sterilizations in the mid-1970s, Jane Lawrence argues:

> the majority [of physicians] ... were white, Euro-American males who believed that they were helping society by limiting the number of births in low-income, minority families.... Some of them did not believe that American Indian and other minority women had the intelligence to use other methods of birth control effectively and that there were already too many minority individuals causing problems in the nation, including the Black Panthers and the American Indian Movement. (410)

Resistance to sterilization has been a defining aspect of Indigenous women's reproductive justice (Silliman et al. 105) and one aspect of their roles as mothers. Governments, in an effort to reduce Indigenous populations, targeted Indigenous women's bodies as the site of surveillance and control, and their capacity as knowledge and history bearers. In conjunction with the removal of Indigenous children from their homes, these attacks created a rupture between generations, between grandmothers, mothers, aunts, and daughters. The Sixties Scoop, that is the removal of Indigenous children from their family of origin and adopted out, closely followed Indigenous women's resistance to sterilization and the closure of residential schools in Canada, another site for the destruction of Indigenous mothering.

RESILIENCE IN THE FACE OF WHITE SETTLER COLONIZATION

In the face of hundreds of years of colonization and oppression, Indigenous peoples have managed to overcome efforts to erase them as the peoples of Turtle Island. Mothers and grandmothers, fathers and grandfathers, and aunts and uncles spoke their stories, and in so doing, they ensured the continuance of narrative ties that link the generations over many centuries, regardless of the residential-industrial school complex. In his text *Education for Extinction*, David Adams writes that among the Indigenous students of the boarding schools, there were "clandestine acts of cultural preservation" (233) enacted through the art of storytelling. He writes that Indigenous children told stories that they had heard from elders. One survivor, Francis La Flesche, recalls how "he and his Omaha friends regularly retreated to a small storeroom, where by candlelight they told stories and ate pemmican secured by secret raids on nearby camps" (qtd. in Adams 233). Another survivor of the boarding school system comments that: "even when we were in school we used to think about our own people and our own ways. [And] someone in the dormitory would start telling a Coyote story" (qtd. in Adams 233). As James Miller argues, "probably the best symbol of Native resistance to the intrusive and oppressive nature of residential schools was found in the persistence of traditional cultural practices, such as dancing among the Plains peoples and potlatch on the Pacific" (372-373). Food was also a site of resistance. Marilyn Iwama writes:

> Removing children from their homes was central to realizing assimilation: confinement interrupted the transmission of culture in each nation. Traditional food practices went underground, and students were nourished by their food only in memory or during family visits. At Christmas or summer vacation, mothers and grandmothers would stuff the little ones with bannock and jam and hot tea and roast meat and potatoes and fresh sweet berries. (244)

Bev Sellars, a survivor of residential schools, writes in her text, *They Called Me Number One,* of the terrible food, often inedible, fed to the children. Children resisted eating the often rotten and spoiled food but were forced to, even though it made some ill. Children learned how to conceal and get rid of inedible food, but this often left them hungry. Sellars writes that they "went on their Sunday walks in the spring and fall ... often stop[ping] to fill our empty bellies with edible plants and berries. We had grown up on the land and had gone with our grandmothers to pick berries and with our grandfathers to hunt" (57). Through food and stories, children resisted assimilation and countered the abuse they experienced in their daily lives in these schools. It was a way to remember their families, their mothers, and their ways of life.

Indigenous women persisted in their mothering in the face of Eurowestern colonialism and its efforts to erase their Indigenous identities, to sterilize Indigenous girls and women, and to remove from them their abilities to share Indigenous knowledge, language, culture, and parenting and reproductive healthcare practices. There was long resistance to colonial efforts to undercut Indigeneity and family relations, but this resistance could not prevent ruptures occurring between families and communities. However, complete erasure and disruption of Indigenous family and community relations could not be realized by white settler governments; instead, Indigenous peoples have storied the atrocities enacted on, and resisted by, them:

> As a mother, Jenny explains: one of the most important tasks that I have undertaken is the role of creating identity in my children.... I have chosen to introduce culture first, and allow this to guide all other aspects of their individual identity. For far too long, my extended and immediate family has had our culture taken away, by banning our culture and the use of our language. I guess you could say that I have turned the tables and made 100% certain that my children have seen and heard and tested every aspect of their cultural identity. And then the other elements of their unique identities can be shaped by their decisions. (qtd. in Kershaw and Harkey 584)

Indigenous women and mothers were cast as improper and unfit in colonial discourses, but it is precisely their Indigenous identities that they have reclaimed and redefined. Indeed, Kim Anderson writes "it was the emotional intelligence of mothering that really transformed me into an Indigenous feminist" (83).

INDIGENOUS FEMINISMS

Although white settler first-wave feminism in the United States drew inspiration from Indigenous women's social, political, economic, and sexual autonomy (Smith, "Native American Feminism" 96-97), many of the first feminists counted themselves among the colonists. If they were sympathetic to Indigenous women, they still tended to see them as less capable in light of being Indigenous. With eugenics dominating Eurowestern white settler societies and Christianity seen as the only spiritual truth, Indigenous systems of belief and practice were cast as pagan and heathen. Christian white settler feminists did not see Indigenous women of Turtle Island as their allies; at best, they were their "wards." Nineteenth and early-twentieth centuries feminists were shaped by both imperialism and colonialism, but more than this, they came to "see themselves as colonizers" (Forestell 10). Locating themselves as colonialists meant that white settler feminists participated in the destruction of Indigenous sociocultural systems: instead of "kill the Indian to save the man" their refrain might have been "kill the 'squaw' to save the woman." It would not be until the second women's movement that white settler feminisms began to act in support of Indigenous women as they struggled against colonial governments.

Wilma Mankiller (1945-2010), of Cherokee background, and Mary Two-Axe Early (b. 1911), a Mohawk woman, are two such Indigenous feminist activists who challenged colonial governments on behalf of Indigenous women. Wilma Mankiller successfully took up the position of chief in a masculinist-oriented band. Her efforts opened the door for young Cherokee women (Mankiller and Wallis 246), whereas Mary Two-Axe Early was among a number of Indigenous women who successfully challenged the gender bias of the Canadian *Indian Act* and secured the passing of the 1985 Bill C-31 (Early 429).

There are, like other feminisms, multiple Indigenous feminisms, but they share certain concerns, such as the impact of colonization. Indigenous feminisms have concerns in common with other racialized feminists in white settler contexts such as, for example, coerced sterilization. Indigenous feminisms also have overlapping concerns with white settler feminisms such as the sexualization of girls and women's bodies. These shared commonalities allow Indigenous feminisms to work in coalition with other feminist groups (Green, "Taking Account of Aboriginal Feminism" 24).

Indigenous feminisms have made apparent—along with black, Chicana, postcolonial, and antiracist feminisms—the necessity to analyze power not only in terms of sexism alone but sexism intersecting with colonialism and racism: "Indian women mobilized a specific discourse of rights from the intersections of human and civil rights, feminism, and Native sovereignty politics to historicize and define their goals to end gender-based discrimination and violence within their communities" (Barker 128-29). This was required, Andrea Smith argues, because

> when an Indigenous woman suffers abuse, this abuse is not just an attack on her identity as a woman but on her identity as an Indigenous woman. The issues of colonial, race, and gender oppression cannot be separated. This explains why, in my experience as a rape crisis counsellor, every Indigenous survivor I have ever counselled said to me at one point, "I wish I was no longer Indian." Women of colour do not just face quantitatively more issues when they suffer violence (that is, less media attention, language barriers, lack of support in the judicial system, etc.) but their experience is qualitatively different from that of white women. (Smith, "Not an Indian Tradition" 71)

White settler, masculine-oriented hegemonies upheld masculine privilege, but this privilege was further defined in terms of whiteness, Christianity, and economic status. To expose particular forms of power, an intersectional analysis was developed and while intersectionality, as method, was developed in a number of different feminist locations, it was most explicitly named by women of colour in the United States. An intersectional analysis, for example, will not ignore differences, as it asks how colonization, racism, and gender intersect so that Indigenous women in Canada and the United States experience higher levels of sexual violence than white settler women. Mary Ellen Kelm writes, following Jean Barman, "sexuality was the crucible of aboriginal-European relations and the source of their most profound contradictions. As the objects of desire and disgust, aboriginal women in the Canadian and US colonial landscapes found themselves in a precarious position" ("Diagnosing the Discursive Indian," 388). The intersecting of gender, colonialism, and race is also evidenced by the significantly higher levels of sterilization experienced by Indigenous women to this day (Briggs et al.). As white settler women marched for access to abortion and the choice to have a child, women of colour and Indigenous women struggled to ensure they could have a child.

A significant aspect of the work of Indigenous feminisms is to expose past and present colonialism, its implications, and the resistance of Indigenous peoples, which includes highlighting both the residential and industrial schools' efforts to erase Indigeneity and the targeting the bodies of girls and women as primary places to further achieve such erasure. Indigenous men, on the other hand, were attacked through their masculinity and seen as ensavaged by their tolerance of the autonomy of Indigenous women. As Shari Huhndorf and Cheryl Suzack write, "For Indigenous women colonization has involved their removal from positions of power, the replacement of traditional gender roles with Western patriarchal practices, the exertion of colonial control over Indigenous communities through the management of women's bodies, and sexual violence" (1). For Indigenous women, reproductive rights include the ability to transmit their culture to their children (Silliman et al. 106).

It is necessary to expose and assess the long history of violence enacted on Indigenous peoples, and often done with recourse to gender and mothering. Dividing Indigenous peoples along the lines of gender (and Indigeneity), and idealizing hierarchy, competition, and dominance were all mechanisms of colonization, even as they were presented as "uplifting" Indigenous peoples. These threads of history are woven through the social fabric of Canada and United States and must be unraveled, closely examined, and then rewoven into stories of strong Indigenous women (Anderson 89). Renate Eigenbrod argues:

> Literature about childhood in residential schools, seemingly

> about victimization, reclaims the power of the imagination in order "to assert our presence in the face of erasure"... thus evoking survival, resistance, and continuance of cultures against colonial policies aimed at the annihilation of Indigenous presence most aggressively in the residential schools. (280)

Shari Huhndorf and Cheryl Suzack indicate that Indigenous feminist incursions in the past allow for reclamation of a denied past, which included women occupying positions of power within their social organizations (1). Examining the past Indigenous feminisms makes apparent that colonization has been gendered and, therefore, requires a gendered analysis (Altamirano-Jimenez 145-146).

Indigenous feminisms also consider the interactions between all life on earth and the interaction between the earth and all life. Indigenous feminist Kim Anderson writes that "Indigenous feminism is linked to a foundational principle in Indigenous societies—that is, the profound reverence for life.... Native Societies, our land-based societies, were much more engaged with ways of honouring and nurturing life—all life" (82). With life, there is also land; thus, Indigenous feminisms also take into account "land rights, sovereignty, and the state's systematic erasure of the cultural practices of native peoples" (Huhndorf and Suzack 6).

A Eurowestern, individual identity has also been imposed on Indigenous peoples in multiple ways—from residential and industrial schools, to the allotment of individual farms under the Dawes Act in the United States (Mankiller and Wallis 5), and to the Indian Act in Canada, which defined who was and was not a so-called Indian. Resisting this narrow vision of identity as singular and alone is a political act of Indigenous feminisms, as is the rejection of a rigid gender ideology that privileges the male over the female, or limits gender to just two kinds. Indigenous women have continued to fight such gender constructions imposed by colonial systems. Wilma Mankiller, for example, a Cherokee chief, wrote that her tribe has begun to return "the balance of the role of women in our tribe," something lost under the pressure of colonialism (Mankiller and Wallis 246).

Returning to this balanced way of life means dealing with sexual violence. Indigenous feminisms address this violence enacted by the state, by groups, and by persons. Violence against Indigenous women is central to the social justice agenda that shape Indigenous feminist practices (Huhndorf and Suzack 7). Andrea Smith argues:

> The reason Native women are constantly marginalized in male-dominated discourses about racism and colonialism and white-dominated discourses about sexism is the inability of both discourses to address the inextricable relationship between gender violence and colonialism. That is, the issue is not simply that violence against women happens during colonization, but that the colonial process is itself structured by sexual violence. Native nations cannot decolonize themselves until they address gender violence, because colonization has succeeded through this kind of violence. ("Introduction" 1)

Indigenous feminisms argue that all Indigenous women have the inherent right to "their body and path in life ... self-governance ... an economic base and resources ... and a distinct identity, history and culture" (Smith, "Native American Feminism" 124-125). Reproductive justice, for Indigenous women, as for women of colour in a racist context, emphasizes "reproductive justice" as opposed to the term "choice" arguing that "choice" obscures the kinds of struggles Indigenous women face (Price).

Andrea Smith argues in her text *Conquest,* the Indigenous (female) body is located as "dirty," "they [Indigenous women] are considered sexually violable and rapable" (9-10), whereas the proper white settler (female) body is "clean" and "pure" and not sexually violable. In the binary oppositional system, two of anything, for example, female and male, are situated in an oppositional relationship with value given to one over and against the other. For example, nature and culture are connected in an oppositional relationship with nature given negative value over again culture, which is given positive value (Juschka). Binary logic, argue Indigenous feminisms, is part of the systemic oppression of Indigenous peoples of Turtle Island.

Indigenous feminisms are multiple, just as white settler or black feminisms are multiple (Huhndorf and Suzack3). Indigenous feminists' insights are shaped by their various locations throughout Turtle Island and by their communities, which are integral to their feminisms. Indigenous feminisms are contextualized in their communities and are neither external nor against them, even if they are critical of their communities. Wilma Mankiller challenged the masculine orientation of the Cherokee band council when she became chief. Doing this, she saw herself having restored the balance that once had been there (Mankiller and Wallis 159, 246). As an Indigenous feminist, Mankiller's agenda of social justice for her people meant that girls too had a chance to enter into the politics of their band councils.

In the neocolonial context of Canada and the United States, the effort to erase Indigenous identities—including the residential-industrial school complex, and the surveillance, control, and sterilization of Indigenous girls and women—have shaped Indigenous mothering in particular and Indigenous parenting in general. Denied Indigenous identity, Indigenous feminists fought back and secured it for themselves and their children. Enclosed in cold, punishing residential and industrial schools, they managed to share stories that helped to sustain their Indigenous identities.

ENDNOTES

[1]Although a two-sex model (that is female and male only) may be at the base of some gender orthodoxies, both female and male are understood to be equivalent or have equal value. This is an ideal and may not have reflected the day-to-day lives of Indigenous peoples. An ideal is that which social relations are mapped out upon, although certainly the ideal emerges from the social body itself. And as with any gender ideology (or any ideology for that matter), there is a dialectal relationship, wherein knowledge shapes the social and the social shapes knowledge and ideology therein.

[2]There were, of course, variations of gender orthodoxy found among colonizers, often shaped by national and religious affiliations, such as British-Anglican, Scottish-Presbyterian, or French Catholic, among others.

[3]In this legal document, "Indian" refers to those who have been recognized as having this status as determined by the Canadian government. I use the term "Indigenous," as it more clearly represents the reality of the landscape of Canada where there are varying degrees of Indigeneity, Metis for example, all of whom were and are affected by the *Indian Act*. The act specifically targeted status Indian women, who lost status if they married nonstatus men, including Métis and Inuit men.

WORKS CITED

Adams, David Wallace. *Education for Extinction: American Indians and the Boarding School Experience 1875–1928*. University Press of Kansas, 1996.

Altamirano-Jimenez. Isabel. "Nunavut: Whose Homeland? Whose Voices." *First Voices: An Aboriginal Women's Reader*, edited by Patricia A Monture and Patricia D. McGuire, Inanna Publications, pp. 143-153.

Anderson, Kim. "Affirmations of an Indigenous Feminist." *Indigenous Women and Feminism: Politics, Activism, Culture*, edited by Cheryl Suzack et al., University of British Columbia Press, 2010, pp. 81-91.

Barker, Joanne. "Gender, Sovereignty, and the Discourse of Rights in Native Women's Activism." *Meridians: Feminism, Race, Transnationalism*, vol. 7, no. 1, 2006, pp. 127-161.

Bourassa, Carrie, et al. "Racism, Sexism, and Colonialism: The Impact on the Health of Aboriginal Women in Canada." *First Voices: An Aboriginal Women's Reader*, edited by Patricia A. Monture and Patricia D. McGuire, Inanna Publications, 2009, pp. 293-304.

Briggs, Laura, et al. "Roundtable: Reproductive Technologies and Reproductive Justice." *Frontiers: A Journal of Women Studies*, vol. 34, no. 3, 2013, pp. 102-125.

Canada, Royal Commission on Aboriginal Peoples, Rene Dussault, and Georges Erasmus. *Report of the Royal Commission on Aboriginal Peoples. Volume 4, Perspectives and Realities*. Federal and Provincial Royal Commissions, Commissions of Inquiry, and Reports, 1996.

Caprio, Myla Vincent. "The Lost Generation: American Indian Women and Sterilization Abuse," *Social Justice*, vol. 31, no. 4, 2004, pp. 40-53.

Carter, Sarah. "Categories and Terrains of Exclusion: Constructing the 'Indian Woman' in Early Settlement Era in Western Canada." *In the Days of Our Grandmothers: A Reader in Aboriginal Women's History in Canada*, edited by Mary-Ellen Kelm and Lorna Townsend. University of Toronto Press, 2006, pp. 146-169.

Chávez-García, Miroslav. "Testing at Whittier School, 1890–1920." *Pacific Historical Review*, vol. 76, no. 2, 2007, pp. 193-228.

de Leeuw, Sarah. "'If Anything Is to Be Done with the Indian, We Must Catch Him Very Young': Colonial Constructions of Aboriginal Children and the Geographies of Indian Residential Schooling in British Columbia, Canada." *Children's Geographies*, vol. 7, no. 2, 2009, pp. 123-140.

de Leeuw, Sarah. "Intimate Colonialisms: The Material and Experienced Places of British Columbia's Residential Schools." *The Canadian Geographer / Le G'Eographe Canadien* vol. 51, no. 3, 2007, pp. 339-358.

Early, Mary Two-Axe. "Indian Rights for Indian Women." *Women, Feminism and Development / Femmes, Féminisme et Développement*, edited by Huguette Dagenais and Denise Piché, McGill-Queen's University Press, 1994, pp. 429-433.

Eigenbrod, Renate. "'For the Child Taken, for the Parent Left Behind': Residential School Narratives as Acts of 'Survivance'." *ESC: English Studies in Canada*, vol. 38, no. 3-4, 2012, pp. 277-297.

Engel, Madeline, et al. "Indigenous Children's Rights." *International Journal of Children's Rights*, vol. 18, no. 2, 2012, pp. 279-299.

Forestell, Nancy. "Mrs. Canada Goes Global: Canadian First Wave Feminism Revisited." *Atlantis*, vol. 30, no. 1, 2005, pp. 7-20.

Green, Joyce. "Balancing Strategies: Aboriginal Women and Constitutional Rights in Canada." *Making Space for Indigenous Feminism*, edited by Joyce Green, Zed Books, 2007, pp. 140-159.

Green, Joyce. "Canaries in the Mines of Citizenship: Indian Women in Canada." *Canadian Journal of Political Science / Revue Canadienne de Science Politique*, vol. 34, no. 4, 2001, 715-738.

Green, Joyce. "Taking Account of Aboriginal Feminism." *Making*

Space for Indigenous Feminism, edited by Joyce Green, Zed Books, 2007, pp. 20-32.

Gurr, Barbara. *Reproductive Justice: The Politics of Health Care for Native American Women.*: Rutgers University Press, 2015.

Henning, Denise. "Yes, My Daughter, We Are Cherokee Women." *Making Space for Indigenous Feminism*, edited by Joyce Green, Zed Books, 2007, pp. 187-198.

Hewitt, Nancy. "Re-rooting American Women's Activism: Global Perspectives on 1848." *Feminist Theory Reader: Local and Global Perspectives*, edited by Carole R. McCann and Seung-kyung Kim, Routledge, 2013, pp. 31-39.

Honouring the Truth, Reconciling for the Future: Summary of the Final Report of the Truth and Reconciliation Commission of Canada. Truth and Reconciliation Commission of Canada, 2015.

Huhndorf, Shari M., and Cheryl Suzack. "Indigenous Feminism: Theorizing the Issues." *Indigenous Women and Feminism: Politics, Activism, Culture*, edited by Cheryl Suzack et al. University of British Columbia Press, 2010, 1-17.

Iwama, Marilyn. "'At Dawn, Our Bellies Full': Teaching Tales of Food and Resistance from Residential Schools and Internment Camps in Canada." *Journal of Intercultural Studies*, vol. 21, no. 3, 2000, pp. 239-254.

Juschka, Darlene. *Political Bodies/Pody politic: The Semiotics of Gender*. Routledge, 2014.

Kelm, Mary-Ellen. "Diagnosing the Discursive Indian: Medicine, Gender, and the 'Dying Race.'" *Ethnohistory*, vol. 52, no. 2, 2005, pp. 371-406.

Kelm, Mary-Ellen. "'A Scandalous Procession': Residential Schooling and the Shaping of Aboriginal Bodies." *Native Studies Review*, vol. 11, no. 2, 1996, 51–88.

Kershaw, Paul, and Tammy Harkey. "The Politics of Power in Care-Giving for Identity: Insights for Indian Residential School Truth and Reconciliation." *Social Politics: International Studies in Gender, State and Society*, vol.18, no. 4, 2011, 572-597.

Lawrence, Jane. "The Indian Health Service and the Sterilization of Native American Women." *American Indian Quarterly*, vol. 24, no. 3, 2000, pp. 400-419.

Mankiller, Wilma, and Michael Wallis. *Mankiller: A Chief and*

Her People. St Martin's Griffin, 1993. Print.

McManus, Sheila. *The Line Which Separates: Race, Gender, and the Making of the Alberta-Montana Borderlands*. University of Nebraska Press, 2005.

Miller, James Robert. *Shingwauk's Vision: A History of Native Residential Schools*. University of Toronto Press, 1996.

Milloy, John S. *A National Crime: The Canadian Government and the Residential School System*. University of Manitoba Press, 1999.

Mosby, Ian. "Administering Colonial Science: Nutrition Research and Human Biomedical Experimentation in Aboriginal Communities and Residential Schools, 1942-1952." *Histoire Sociale/ Social History*, vol. 46, no. 91 2013, 145-172.

Moss, Erin L., et al. "From Suffrage to Sterilization: Eugenics and the Women's Movement in 20th Century Alberta." *Canadian Psychology*, vol. 54, no. 2, 2013, pp. 105-114.

Pegoraro, Leonardo. "Second-Rate Victims: The Forced Sterilization of Indigenous Peoples in the USA and Canada." *Settler Colonial Studies*, vol. 5, no. 2, 2015, pp. 161-173.

Perdue, Theda. *Cherokee Women: Gender and Cultural Change 1700–1835*. Univeristy of Nebraska Press, 1998.

Pisciotta, Alexander. "Race, Sex, and Rehabilitation: A Study of Differential Treatment in the Juvenile Reformatory, 1825–1900." *Crime and Delinquency*, vol. 29, no. 2, 1983, pp. 254-269.

Price, Kimala. "What Is Reproductive Justice?" *Meridians: Feminism, Race, Transnationalism* 10.2 (2010): 42–65. Print.

Ralstin-Lewis, D. Marie. "The Continued Struggle Against Genocide: Indigenous Women's Reproductive Rights." *Wicazo Sa Review*, vol. 20, no. 1, 2005, 71-95.

Roscoe, Will. *Changing Ones: Third and Fourth Genders in Native North America*. St. Martin's Press, 1998.

Savage, Candace. *A Geography of Blood: Unearthing Memory from a Prairie Landscape*.: Greystone Books, 2012.

Sellars, Bev. *They Called Me Number One: Secrets and Survival at an Indian Residential School*. Talon Books, 2013.

Shoemaker, Nancy. "Introduction." *Negotiators of Change: Historical Perspectives on Native American Women*, edited by Nancy Shoemaker, Routledge, 1995, pp. 1-25.

Silliman, Jael, et al. *Undivided Rights: Women of Color Organize for Reproductive Justice*. South End Press, 2004.

Smith, Andrea. *Conquest: Sexual Violence and American Indian Genocide*. South End Press, 2005.

Smith, Andrea. *Indigenous Peoples and Boarding Schools: A Comparative Study*. Secretariat of the United Nations, Permanent Forum on Indigenous issues, 2008.

Smith, Andrea. "Introduction: Native Women and State Violence." *Social Justice*, vol. 31, no. 4, 2004), 1-7.

Smith, Andrea. "Native American Feminism: Sovereignty and Social Change." *Making Space for Indigenous Feminism*, edited by Joyce Green, Zed Books, 2007, pp. 93-107.

Smith, Andrea. "Not an Indian Tradition: The Sexual Colonization of Native Peoples." *Hypatia, Indigenous Women in the Americas*, vol. 18, no. 2, 2003, pp. 70-85.

Stote, Karen. "The Coercive Sterilization of Aboriginal Women in Canada." *American Indian Culture and Research Journal*, vol. 36, no. 3, 2012, pp. 117-150.

Stubblefield, Anna. "'Beyond the Pale': Tainted Whiteness, Cognitive Disability, and Eugenic Sterilization." *Hypatia*, vol. 22, no. 2, 2007, pp. 162-181.

Williams, Trevor John. "Compulsive Measures: Resisting Residential Schools at One-Arrow Reserve, 1889–1896." *The Canadian Journal of Native Studies*, vol. 34, no. 2, 2014, pp. 197-222.

3.
Reclaiming Indigenous Practices in a Modern World

CARRIE BOURASSA

THIS CHAPTER EXPLORES my personal experiences of becoming an Indigenous mother as well as traditional mothering and parenting practices. It will employ Indigenous storytelling methodology (Kovach) to explore the following questions: How can we be traditional Indigenous mothers in this contemporary, fast-paced world? What does it mean to be a traditional Indigenous mother? Can traditional practices, such as Berry Fasts, for young women be passed on in urban settings? How do we have "real" conversations with our children in this digital age? Why is ceremony integral to reclamation of Indigeneity? Elder Betty McKenna helps to explore these questions based on her traditional *Anishinaabe* and Métis teachings. She also shares traditional understandings of mothering and parenting practices and her understanding of the centrality of these in the reclamation process.

I am *Ts'iotaat Kutx Ayanaha s'eek* (Morning Star Bear). I wish I was raised with my traditions, but I wasn't. I know that this is common in our communities—all too common. I remember when I began my reclamation process as a young woman. My kookum, Elder Betty McKenna, once said to me: "We are like trees. Our roots are put down very deep. And we take things from the four directions and we take them into our lives. And if you pull us up by the roots, we are lost. We have to go back and find those roots; find those beginnings that are strong so that we can live a good life."

When I became a mother, the concept of identity became particularly important to me. I had spent years reclaiming my identity. I had to come to terms with the loss of my identity through intergenerational trauma, violence, and abuse. I had to understand the intergenerational effects of colonization on my family and how historical trauma works. Although I confess that I continue to learn each day about these processes and effects, I now understand that healing is a journey, not a destination. I am at a point where I feel comfortable in my skin, something I never thought would happen. But having children really makes you think about your identity. For me, it made me think about how I could possibly pass on traditions that I never grew up with. How could I reclaim my Indigeneity and also pass it on to my children? And how could I do this in an urban context? After all, I didn't know about Indigenous mothering or parenting practices. But I wanted to. I desperately wanted to. Something deep inside my soul told me that they were there, inherently ingrained in me, somewhere in my DNA. That's the thing about attempted genocide. They can't get to your spirit.

So I began another phase of my journey to reclamation. At the time when I seriously began thinking about these questions, my eldest daughter, Victoria, who is now seventeen, was only five. I remember when she was still in my womb; she was very responsive to the beat of the drums. I was still very much in the midst of my healing journey. Although I know that I am still healing and always will be, I was going through a particularly hard time just as I became pregnant with her. I was constantly drawn to the healing beat of the drum and my unborn daughter was as well. She would kick to the beat of the drum—always in perfect rhythm with it. After she was born, she began attending ceremony with me, and it was apparent from a young age that she had incredible gifts. She spent a great deal of time with kookum Betty. By the time my daughter was five, she attended her first sweat and was gifted with her first name *La Tete Ayikis Quay* (Head Frog Woman).

I must confess that I was in the midst of my PhD, and my thoughts of traditional parenting practices were reduced to attending ceremony when we could. When we could, my daughter had gotten into the habit of taking her tobacco pouch wherever she went and would often put tobacco down even if she was just going to pick a dandelion. She also got into the habit of telling other children they should be putting tobacco down because Mother Earth is sacred. I was proud but consumed with our fast-paced, instant-everything lifestyle. I was juggling my PhD studies, a new faculty appointment, and felt this intense need to succeed. I didn't want to let my family or community down, and to be honest, I felt that I had to prove myself. I still feel that way most days—another colonial remnant that many of us have to find a way to discard.

After I had my second daughter, Lillie, my life began to shift. She was a big surprise and blessing. I have lupus, and we struggled to have more children after Victoria. When Lillie was born, I began to once again think about the idea of Indigenous mothering. I started to speak to kookum Betty about it and began slowly. The first thing I did was breastfeed. This is something that was not advised when I had Victoria because of the medications I was on for my lupus. However, more is now known about lupus, and my doctors encouraged breastfeeding. Breastfeeding may not be for everyone, and I did have to supplement, but for me, it was an incredible bonding experience with Lillie. Kookum Betty spoke of the many traditional practices when babies are born into Anishinaabe communities:

> We do things for the mother after the baby is born ... how you clean the mother after that baby is born. You use sweetgrass water to bathe her, and there are things that father has to do before that baby is born to encourage her to have breast milk and that's the father's part to bring the mother nutritious soup so that she can nurse that child. And there's also the mother needs to have that time to just be with their babies ... nowadays we see young women in the mall with their babies and you say "how old is it" and they'll say "four days old"... that never happened way back when because that baby doesn't know ... it's confused; it doesn't know where it's supposed to be. It used to be put in a mossbag and it was strapped to the mom and it heard her heartbeat and her breathing and was with its mom for the longest time. And those things I think, those are things that we are say are Indigenous—those are Indigenous ways of being with your child. Same with your child's umbilical cord and having it placed in a little medicine bag or taking the

> afterbirth and placing it in mother earth so the child is always connected to mother earth—those are things that are Indigenous. And if we don't go back to the whole concept of indigenizing our life then we'll constantly have people who are wandering around not knowing they have a connection to Mother Earth.

Kim Anderson notes that umbilical cords signify the unity between the child and his or her family and kin. Her research reveals that in some nations, the mother and child take the navel cord bag and bury it in the woods at the end of the first year of the child's life. This action signifies that it is time for the child to develop as an individual, whereas in other nations the mother keeps the navel cord and gives it to the child when he or she gets older. In other nations, moreover, the navel cord is attached to a moss bag or around the child's neck. Anderson's research also reveals that cradleboards and mossbags are often used for babies. She notes that "The Anishinaabek saw cradleboards as a way of developing the child's physical and mental capacities" (*Life Stages* 59). Children would also learn to self-soothe and would learn their daily routines (Anderson, *Life Stages*). Breastfeeding was a common practice not only because of nutrition but also for bonding. Anderson notes that children often breastfed until they were four or five years old. Breastfeeding practices were disrupted in the 1950s as public health nurses pressured mothers to use bottles and cow's milk (Anderson).

Although I had been continuing with ceremony, I wanted to bring ceremony into the home. I had to take the girls and travel out to the land, and although I love to do this, sometimes, life gets in the way. I wanted to be able to bring ceremony into our everyday lives in an urban setting. Kookum Betty says, "That's who we are—ceremony. I can't separate my life from ceremony. Without ceremony I have no life without life I have no ceremony."

A few daily things that we began doing was smudging in the morning and evening. Smudging is a cleansing of the mind, body, and spirit. You can burn sweetgrass, sage, or a combination of sacred medicines to cleanse or purify yourself in preparation for prayer. We also began putting tobacco out on Mother Earth. When

I asked kookum Betty how I could bring ceremony into my life. She said all women and all mothers can do this:

> What I'd like to say to young women is to be brave and to be dedicated. What I mean is it takes a lot of bravery to say "I can do this." You might want to do it once, or twice ... you know that feeling when you start something "oh this is cool, this is neat" but if you've got to put that into practice every day it might be easy to fall into your old way of life "I'm too busy to do this, I'm too busy to do that." But take one thing that you find that's good in our culture ... say I'll speak to the Creator everyday and put down that tobacco offering. Just do that one thing, start doing that one thing today, start putting that offering down every day and instead of just doing it quickly, do it purposely and touch Mother Earth with that offering and things will change in your life. That one small thing every day and things will change and begin to grow, and you will get stronger and stronger because it does take a long time for things to come into your life. No matter how good it is, people are going to be pressed for time, and they'll go back to their old ways of doing things, but if you want your children to learn from you, that's how you do it. You start small. And I'd have to say that's how you bring ceremony into your life. And there, it just grows from there.

My eldest has her own smudge pot, sage, and tobacco. I would say for a teenager, she is fairly consistent. She understands the meaning behind it, and I know she is struggling with something when I see her out with her tobacco or smell the sage burning. Sometimes Lillie and I coax her out with us to put tobacco down. She is learning, and I am proud. Lillie is very dedicated. Every morning I hear "Mama we 'mudge now? Mama we put 'bacco out now?" This is our routine, and it nourishes my spirit.

There are more routines now; they have been part of reclaiming Indigeneity, not only for me but also for my girls. When Victoria turned twelve, she had her first moon time (menses). I approached kookum Betty, as I knew there was a traditional ceremony to launch young women into the rapids of life according to Anishinaabe tradition, and she told me the following:

> Well, we can't have a moon lodge like it used to be ... when women had their first moon time they would go into the moon lodge for fourteen days ... aunties and grandmas would follow you, and they would teach you how to clean yourself and how to take care of yourself at that time and give you teachings, how to wash yourself properly and there was, were women ways that you needed to know. And there were many stories teaching us those practices as well. But you can't take fourteen days now for a child, you can't take them out of school ... you just, the school wouldn't stand for it ... and some say "well do it in the summer" well you can't, you have to do it at their first moon time. So when they went into that moon lodge, you had to have your own plates, fork, knife, spoon, cups and no one else ate off it, just you because you're on your moon time, so you're powerful, so you want to keep that power to yourself. You didn't want someone eating from your plate so they didn't get the benefit of the food they were eating because you were just too powerful. So even if it was washed that power was still there and that power goes to that young woman because she is going into that time of being a life giver and that's a lot of power. That's, you know, you're a copy of Mother Earth and Mother Earth is very, very powerful.

So we had a beautiful ceremony at the full moon, where Victoria's first moon time was celebrated and she would begin her year-long Berry Fast. According to Anishinaabe teachings, young women begin their Berry Fast after their first moon time. Puberty fasts are common among many tribal nations. Anderson notes that they vary across nations and are different for boys and girls. Boys often undertake vision quests, whereas girls have different ceremonies often honouring their moon time.

Kookum Betty reflected on Victoria's Berry Fast:

> That was a very special time for the community to welcome her into that space when she done her Berry Fast for them to see this young girl have the courage to go through that ceremony and know that she had been asked four times, "Do you want to do this? Do you want to do this?" and she did it, you know? And I think for her too it was a self-realization that she wasn't her father, she wasn't her mother, and she was her own person. She wasn't influenced by friends around her to do it, but it was just in her and the strength that the Creator gave her and the resolve that she had to take that into her own life and then being able to take as I say "traditional," good, knowledgeable ceremony and bring it to a child in the twenty-first century. This young lady was able to go through that ceremony the same way people had done for thousands of years in her community amongst people who loved her and cared for her, amongst people she had respect for, and she also clearly understood the importance of going through that Berry Fast and the sacrifice she was making for that year of not having berries. I think she understood it a lot better than her parents did. And I think that when she undertook those things she would do and when she stood with her ancestors under the full moon, and they were there, they were supporting her and stood on either side of her [and] that was so cool and she saw that they were there—and I think that gave her the strength to draw on—I think she went back to that night all throughout that year and drew on the strength of that night thinking "they were there with me, I can do this," "they were there with me, I can do this" that ... that was her way of doing it.

Victoria fasted for a full year. Indeed, she did understand the significance more than her father and I did. Many times we forgot that she could not have berries and would offer her blueberry muffins or strawberry smoothies, but she never wavered. Over the course of the year, she started to understand clearly the significance of giving up berries as she began to deal with the pressures of her peers in school. She understood that if she could give up berries, she could also abstain from alcohol, drugs, and sex. I was amazed at her transformation over the course of a year. She had transformed into a young woman and no longer was my little girl. At the end of the year, kookum Betty held a sweat to end her Berry Fast and to launch her into the rapids of life. She was given important teachings and gifts including her new name *La Tete Ayikis Quay* (Head Frog Woman). As Kookum Betty explained it,

> So nowadays, I gave her [Victoria] a little set of dishes because normally in the moon lodge within so many days everyone in the moon lodge would be on their moon time—your sisters, your aunts.... So her set of dishes is not only for herself but if her friends came over instead of one dish, one cup, one fork, one spoon she got a set of dishes, so if she had friends over, and she was on her moon time, she could serve them. She could use those plates exclusively for her when she was on her moon time or if you and she were on your moon time together, you and she could eat off those plates. That's what it was all about, and she got instructions about that and also that she was to wash her clothes, everything, T-shirts, jeans, could be washed with yours but can't be washed with her dad's. And also giving her the teaching of the other gifts she was given at that time. Her birch bark scrolls that she had her [hand and foot] prints on, she knows that has a special place for her and for her father; that is a special bond for her and her dad for many years to come. And of course her claw, her bear claw, to give her that strength of the bear, and she will become a strong mother and have strong mothering skills. She will be a strong mother, whether they are her own children or other's children. That instinct will be there to be a mother and that is a traditional practice.

It is our role as parents, grandparents, aunties, uncles, and extended family and community to provide Victoria with the seven stones that she needs as she navigates the rapids of life from the ages of thirteen to emerge from the rapids at age twenty. The stones that we need to give her to hold include growth, adequacy, love, order, social approval, security, and self-esteem. If youth don't get these stones during these years, they will seek false stones and that is when our youth get into trouble. That is when addictions, for example, can take hold and this can prevent them from emerging from the rapids. Our communities have many adults who are still "in the rapids." As Elder Danny Musqua states,

> Every stage of childhood was a celebration because children needed to develop a sense of belonging; that sense that you are important to people. If a child doesn't have a sense of belonging and responsibility as part of a whole, that's the weakness that will tear up a community. That's the weakness that the child will have in later years, in times of great need or difficulty. (qtd. in Anderson, *Life Stages* 65)

Although ceremonies may change to adapt to contemporary environments, the purpose and intent remain the same. Kookum Betty reflected on this adaption when talking about Victoria's Berry Fast:

> And long ago the ceremony was perhaps a little different; we didn't have all the things we had there that night. We didn't have plastic chairs that we had in the circle as we were waiting for her to come down and enter the circle. But she traditionally was able to take the ceremony on the buffalo robe that had been done for thousands of years. That's traditional. She had her hand and foot prints on birch bark. That's traditional. We were able to bring that to her. The berries were served in plastic bowls instead of birch bark bowls, but they were still berries, natural and wild, and were the berries that she should be eating. And the sacred fire was there, made with love and care by her uncles who built it for her, and her aunties came to be there as well. And for her to wear her bear claw ... that is the way it had been for thousands of years. The community surrounding that little girl, surrounded her with that care and love, and put her into that space. We did a few things different nowadays, we light the sacred fire with a match, we had plastic bowls, we had cameras,

> but we do still have the traditional drums, we have the traditional songs from thousands of years-ago, and still have Grandmother Moon shining down upon us. So in many ways, we live in a world that we say is the twenty-first century but take away the plastic, and take away the wooden matches and the modern-day clothes that people were wearing, and it was like it was a thousand years ago, and we had it in our hearts the way it was a thousand years ago. And then when she came out from that ceremony and had the strength to say to other girls in school "well I can't have berries because I'm on a berry fast," that took strength for her to say. She faced ridicule at times, but she faced it down and said that's not me. It's not going to take away what I'm doing. There's strength in that, and of course there's a lot of temptations out in this world now. No matter where she looks or what time of the year you can get berries now; every store, every drive-in there's berry ice cream, there's berry floats, you name it, you know? But she was still able to push it aside and say no. We didn't have those temptations a thousand years ago ... we didn't have those temptations when I went through it. We didn't have those things—you either had it when it was in season or you didn't have it all, so there were no blueberry muffins or cakes and those types of things, so in a sense it was an easier time. Nowadays, she needed all those prayers and that strength to get through that because there were a lot of temptations in her way. She still made it, and I think the way she conducts herself now, she's gone through that, so she knows she has the strength in many, many things, many things.

Part of our routine has been that Victoria and I wash our clothes separately from my husband's and Lillie's when we are on our moon time. Victoria uses her cups, plates, forks, and spoons when she is on her time and washes them separately. We don't cook for others when we are on our time. We respect and honour the gift we have as women. For Victoria, this is how she has grown up, and it is natural to her. She is growing up to be a proud Indigenous woman. For me, these are new teachings, and I have welcomed the opportunity to learn them with my daughter. I am comforted knowing that my daughters will be raised with these teachings and will be able to pass them on to their children. They will not need to reclaim them.

Although our routines have been enriched through the help of kookum Betty, I have often wondered what it was like long ago. What did traditional Indigenous mothering look like? I sat and listened as kookum Betty shared her knowledge.

> I can tell you what it was. Mothering wasn't done just by one person, and it's certainly not done by the one person who gives birth to someone because you can mother someone without giving birth to someone. That's what the aunties and the grandmothers in our communities have done. Some of them were not related to us at all, but they were still our aunties and our grandmothers. And aunties and grandmothers played such an important role in the mothering process for us because mothering really is a state of being that allows the nurture and care for things and others. And it is how you learn about yourself, you learn your way of being as part of that mothering system whether you were a boy or a girl.
>
> You see boys would stay with their mothers until they were twelve years old and then they would go off with their fathers to do the hunting and fishing and other things, but until that time, as I can recall, our aunties would teach us things like how to be with our mothers. It's something that's really missing in this day and age with our children that they don't know how to be with their mothers. We learnt that there was a part that we played to keep our mothers ... I don't want to say happy, but the way we treated our mothers and spoke to our mothers was a gentle way and they'd teach us that .... and if you stepped out of that line of not being gentle then they would teach you not to. You know don't raise your voice to your mother, don't speak back to your mother, don't ever hit your mother. You know even as a young child, you see an eighteen-month-old child

> they're on their mother's knee—I've witnessed this myself nowadays—where a child will just smack their mother or they will say "no" to their mother. We learnt from our aunties and grandmothers that that's not an acceptable; we have to learn how to take care of the life giver who brought us into this world.
>
> So that is all a part of mothering and nurturing because as you grow up with those values as a mother yourself, you then learn that you do not do that to your child either. You don't speak loudly to them, you don't slap them; it's not harsh discipline. There is a way of being able to live with your mother and your mother living with you that was part of natural learning. There's that natural process that your mother would let you learn, by that process without stepping in to stop you because you would never be a whole person if she did. So if you were playing with a baby for instance and they would drop something—say they dropped a toy and they would want that toy—rather than the mother picking up that toy and putting it back on the chair with the child, she would let that child go through that process of crying and wanting that toy. Her role was not to pick that toy up and put it on the chair. You soon learnt as a child that if you wanted to play with something you kept it there on the chair, you did not drop it. And there were very young children that learned that. I've seen my younger brothers and sisters learn that as well.
>
> That's a "learning," and once you're brought into this world, once you come through that door way everything you do in life is a "learning." You copy other people around us. So if you have a mother nowadays who will holler at her child or slap her child, she doesn't realize she's teaching that child to slap others and to slap someone smaller than themselves, someone who's younger and defenseless. So it's a learned behaviour; it does not come naturally.

Her words had me reflecting about three things. One was the notion of extended family and community. It was not just my job or my husband's job to raise our girls, but, in fact, it was important for them to have a variety of people involved in their upbringing. In that moment, I was grateful not only for our daughters' blood relatives but also for their kin—aunties, uncles, and for kookum Betty—who all have played and will continue to play such integral roles in their lives. I was very blessed to have this in an urban setting, but I know this is more difficult for others. I know from conversations with my students that when you are displaced from your home community it can be difficult to find support systems and expand your kin network. However, I also know that Indigenous urbanization is increasing and that we need to support one another and help build those much needed networks and support systems wherever we decide to live.

Anderson's research supports kookum Betty's teachings. She finds that among many nations, children have never been beaten, and only rarely reprimanded; they have been taught by example *(Life Stages)*. According to Leah Dorion, who conducted research with Cree and Metis elders in Saskatchewan, "one is not to interfere with the sacred covenant between the Creator and another being or there will be negative consequences" (qtd. in Anderson, *Life Stages* 68). Children have been taught to be disciplined, self-reliant, and interdependent, beliefs that have been fostered through the practices of noninterference (Anderson, *Life Stages*).

The second notion I had was how do we interact with our children and grandchildren in this high-tech, fast-paced world if we are trying to be traditional mothers? How does that work? My eldest has her iPhone with her at all times and it is, in fact, her main mode of communication. Kookum Betty was very pragmatic in response:

> You know what? I use that stuff. That's how I contact those kids. You go to where they're learning. You go to where they're living. A long time ago, it was auntie or grandma taking us for a walk, you know, but you can text that person, you can, you can Facebook that person. There's so many ways that you can use that technology to reach those young minds now. If they're in the blueberry bush then go to the blueberry bush and sit and talk to them, you know? If they're at a protest march, go march with them. That's

> how we have real conversations with them, so make it work for you. There's no such thing as a bad thing as opposed to a good thing; there's just a thing. Technology is in our lives for a reason, so we need to learn to use those things to advance our cause as human beings, and if we want to survive as human beings, it starts with the life givers.

Finally, the last notion I was reflecting on was what traditional Indigenous mothering actually meant. I was pondering on the idea, so I asked kookum Betty about it. She shared her thoughts:

> I think one of the things we need to do is get rid of the concept of "traditional"; a lot of the young people think traditional means old, and it's not. We need to think of it as "good" knowledge, but I would take traditional out and call it "good" knowledge. And with good knowledge, there are many ways you can do it. I still believe that people being together creating a place—a time, a space, a place—where you can bring people together and enjoy one another's company. They can bounce ideas off one another, they can learn a good way of life, and they can pick up this good knowledge, put it into their life and incorporate in their world their own way. It has to become theirs. It can't be somebody else's that they're trying to fit their world around; they have to be able to put it into their life and find the goodness there for themselves.

These words rang true to me as I remembered her once saying that we must also never judge each other. She said, "There is no right or wrong way, just a way." In writing about "traditional" or good Indigenous mothering, there is no intent to judge anyone but merely to share experiences that may be common to others so that we can support each other. That is what Indigenous feminism is about. We need to (re)define these words that have been defined for us. Dawn Martin-Hill writes about the construct of "traditional" women who are subservient to men who "never questions male authority ... she is quiet, she prays, she obeys, she raises the children, she stays home, she never questions or challenges domination—she is subservient" (108). She describes how Indigenous women have had "traditional" defined and constructed for us. But according to her nation, the Haudenosaunee, the women work in the fields, harvest, and prepare the foods and clothing; children are raised by the matrilineal family and extended family, and the mother's brothers are also responsible for childrearing (Martin-Hill). As kookum Betty said, childrearing is a communal responsibility.

How do we (de)construct these words and identities? We do it little by little. We must be strong in our own identities as women and mothers, aunties, sisters, grandmothers. Martin-Hill notes that the "project of decolonization today is to reclaim what has become lost in our recent history: the values, beliefs and practices of Sacred Woman" (111). In my family's case, we have done this over many years beginning with my own reclamation process, and as kookum Betty suggested, started small. Ceremonies, no matter how big or small, are essential aspects of that (de)construction and reclamation process. As Anderson notes, "In past times (as in many communities yet today), ceremonies were important in building the relationships (human, animal and spirit) that would be necessary to maintain a lifetime of good health and well-being" (*Life Stages*, 38). Kookum Betty shared the following:

> Our people believed drawing breath was a sacred ceremony because you come from water to breathing ... that's a sacred ceremony to take that air into your lungs ... that you should see the value in breathing every day. That is the sacredness of who I am and the sacredness of that spark of the Creator that's within me and that ability to draw life into my lungs. So I breathe it in, I breathe it out; to me that's a ceremony.

The idea of "drawing breath as a sacred ceremony" is an important one. The processes of colonization have taken place over hundreds of years and over many generations. Some argue that it has not ended. Neocolonialism continues as policies and legislation target Indigenous people and control our lives. Canada remains one of the few countries in the world that continues to define its Indigenous people in legislation. This on its own causes identity confusion, loss, and displacement within families and communities. Martin-Hill notes that "we must rebuild our relationships together as women and learn to respect one another's sacred spaces" (118). She contends that we must see ourselves as sacred women and mothers. Assuming traditional roles as mothers may mean different things to each of us, but she points out that mothers were essentially teachers, whereas children were taught and raised collectively. So however you choose to carry that out in today's modern-day, fast-paced world is up to you. What is important is that we take reclaim our identities—our sacredness. We are the carriers of our culture (Anderson, "Affirmation"). It is our responsibility to share it with our children, even if we do so by learning it with them and by reclaiming it with them.

Anderson reminds us that "Motherhood, both in practice and as an ideology, was the source of Indigenous female authority in the family and in the governance of our pre-colonial nations. Contemporary Indigenous peoples now call on these teachings as part of the political discourse related to healing and rebuilding" ("Affirmations" 86). Colonization affected gender roles and relations and continues to today. Unfortunately, patriarchy still dominates in many of our communities, and women's roles are often not valued beyond childbearing. For mother's roles to be truly valued, men must honour mother's roles in their entirety not merely for our ability to give birth. We must expect more of our men and reclaim our roles, our identities, as the sacred woman and mother.

WORKS CITED

Anderson, Kim. *Life Stages and Native Women: Memory, Teachings, and Story Medicine*. University of Manitoba Press, 2011.

Anderson, Kim. "Affirmations of an Indigenous Feminist", *Indigenous Women and Feminism: Politics, Activism and Culture*, edited by Cheryl Suzack et al., University of British Columbia Press, 2010, pp. 81-91.

Martin-Hill, Dawn. "Colonial Constructs of the 'Traditional Woman.'" *Strong Woman Stories: Native Vision and Community Survival*, edited by Kim Anderson and Bonita Lawrence, Sumach Press, 2003, pp. 106-120.

4.
Nîso-okâwimâwak (Two Mothers)

JANET SMYLIE AND NANCY COOPER

IN THIS CHAPTER, we share in first-person narrative the ways that as urban Indigenous lesbians, we weave together a family fabric of traditional and modern Indigenous knowledge and practice. We focus on the process of planning for pregnancy, being pregnant, birthing, and mothering our twins Jay and Quinn, who are now eight and who were conceived in a process that took two years and involved a dear friend, who is a gay Indigenous man and now their dad. The process included ceremony, trials of home insemination, a courier service, and a fertility clinic. We had Indigenous and allied midwives as well as obstetric care and a birth story that included a medicine pouch, emergency surgery, and a traditional welcoming ceremony. Our parenting to date has involved lots of aunties, uncles, cousins, and grandparents, ceremonies, sleepless nights, endless learning (by both moms and boys), and a million joyful moments. Jay and Quinn feel very special for having such a big family. Our stories follow below beginning with one of the two mothers, Janet Smylie.

WHERE I COME FROM

On my mother's side, I come from a long line of strong and resilient Métis and First Nations people. My "half-breed" lineage spans seven generations and what is now known as Manitoba, Alberta, Saskatchewan, and Ontario—roughly in that order.

These days, Louis Riel is celebrated as a national hero. The fact that he was demonized in the national press and that the Métis and First Nations peoples he mobilized were commonly regarded by European settlers in Eastern Canada as primitive traitors who were impeding the spread of civilization is often forgotten by the ancestors of these settlers and those who have come after. But not by my people.

After rebelling, resisting, and then finally losing a lopsided battle with a colonizing nation that had a self-serving agenda of "settling" our land base with European newcomers, many of my ancestors learned to be careful about disclosing or discussing their Métis ancestry to outsiders. In the trials and persecutions of Métis that followed their defeat at the Battle of Batoche, this "hiding" of identity might have meant the difference between life and death, freedom and imprisonment. In the decades that followed, persistent anti-Métis stigma could easily translate into the loss of job and educational opportunities or into social isolation.

My grandma, who was born on a road allowance[1] in Alberta in 1918, used to say when I asked about my ancestry, "You come from good people—and that's all you need to know." The youngest of ten children, her mother died when she was two, and she spent her childhood moving around the prairies living with different family members. She was unmarried and still young when she got pregnant with my mother. For this, she was excommunicated from the Catholic Church. The story is that the nuns tried to bribe her with pain medication during labour in exchange for agreeing to let my mother be taken away from her for adoption after birth. She didn't give in.

Growing up in Ontario, outside of our historic homeland, I always knew I was "part Indian." No need for a Supreme Court fight about this from my perspective. Before she died, my mother Mavis taught us children about respect—imprinting us with a strong sense of social humility and social justice. She was known in the small town I grew up in as someone who spoke up and told you directly what she thought. As a child, I didn't know that being part Indian was something that I might be shamed for. In fact, I can recall vividly one of the first times that this entered into my conscious awareness. I was in grade four or five, and we were studying "the Indians of Canada." I put up my hand and stated confidently "I am part Indian" and the teacher asked me, "East or West?" I didn't understand the question, and the class broke out into laughter.

As a young woman, I realized that I needed to know more about the good people from whom I came. In medical school, I reached out to family and went to the archives in Ottawa to do some research. Of course, it is the names of the white and "half-breed" men that are easier to track over the course of time, so I know that in the late 1700s a white man named James Peter Whitford arrived from England and married a Saulteaux woman, who was simply named Sarah in the English papers. My family's "half-breed" script isn't much better at telling me the story of my maternal kin line. I try to imagine between the lines of her "half-breed" script. What was it like for my grandmother's great-grandmother Nancy, who is described as formerly taking Treaty as part of the "Edmonton Stragglers" band, to sign away her treaty rights with an X for forty-seven dollars? One of my aunties, who has a way of making you feel better about things, told me when I self-consciously showed her my squirrelled-away photocopies late one evening that the "Stragglers" were actually some of the most resilient survivors on the prairies at the time of treaty making—as good hunters and gatherers, they avoided starvation for longer and hence "straggled in" after most people had already taken treaty.

Luckily, I live in a time where, thanks to the hard work of many before me, history and its associated biases are being revisited. I do face challenges, big and small, which I attribute to racism, particularly within academic institutions. For example, a senior university administrator (now retired) once announced at a research meeting I was leading that Métis are "angry, disorganized, and hard to work with." I have been routinely questioned about my identity, "Indian status," and blood quantum by both settlers and Indigenous people who don't understand Métis kinship and history. Fortunately, my father, my mother, and my stepmother nurtured in me an intellectual self-confidence, work ethic, and tenacity that allow me to stand my ground. And unlike my mother, grandmother, and ancestors before them, for the most part, I haven't had to fear for my livelihood by asking questions, doing research, and celebrating who I am as a Métis woman.

The trail of Métis kinship has become easier to travel, but it is not completely clear. And as a Métis mother, I know that the continuity of kinship between past and future generations is one of the most important gifts I can pass onto my children. For we live most fully in the present knowing where we have come from and where we are going. This is the story of how I have tried to nurture *wahkohtowin* or "all my relations" for my boys Jay and Quinn. This is what cultural continuity means to me.

NURTURING MOTHER-SPARK

As an Indigenous woman who has travelled a lot, I have always found something grounding and reassuring about beaches and tides. Ocean tides, echoing the rocky driftwood lakeshores of my childhood in which cloud shadowed whitecaps whipped and warned and sometimes swallowed those who dared test them, remind me that I am but a miniscule and finite part of something much bigger and powerful.

Irrefutable proof of the pull of the moon, the breakers stir up mother-spark inside me—an old-new desire to nurture and create that has survived despite frayed and sometimes broken kin lines, relationship breakup, and internalized belief that I will not be good at this. My adoptive mother sits with me and fuels this fire with love and recognition. She understands this pull. She did it on her own in the middle of overwhelming grief, and then built up our makeshift family that now we say accepts all comers. There is never a perfect time to have a baby. It is imperfectly perfect.

WEAVING FAMILY

Just as I was confirming my intention and resolve to become a mother with or without a partner, I received an email from an old friend. I was living in Ottawa. Nancy, who lived in Toronto at that time, usually connected with me once or twice a year for lunch along with a mutual mentor when they came into Ottawa for their Indigenous literacy work. We had met many years before this in Toronto. I had heard on the relatively small two-spirit grapevine that Nancy had been single for a little while. I had always admired her strength and commitment to community, not to mention her beautiful and attractive presence.

This invite seemed a bit different from the others—when she contacted me this time, she proposed dinner in lieu of lunch and there was no mention of a third party. After some back and forth email, I was pretty certain this was actually a first date. We joke now because she still claims that her intentions were perhaps more innocent than mine.

A few months later and seriously in love, we still had a few relationship logistics to work through. I was leaving to start a new job in Saskatchewan, and it seemed a bit too soon for Nancy to follow me out from Toronto—unlike some of my family members. Nancy and I have experienced contrasting styles of communication in our families of origin. I joke that my rapid response communication style is an attempt to belie stereotypes about Indigenous peoples having long pause times. When my family gets together, we are quite animated and excited, and tend to talk a lot—sometimes at the same time. It can be hard to get a word in edgewise. The first time Nancy met my extended family, at a pre-Christmas gathering, was no exception. At one point my sister, excited about the idea that my nephew might eventually have a new cousin, asked me, in front of Nancy, if I wanted to pick up his old crib and take it out west with me. Clearly overwhelming to Nancy at the time, this became known as the "crib incident." Luckily, she stuck it through.

BUILDING *WAHKOHTOWIN* IN A MODERN FAMILY WAY

They say that lesbians have worked through a lot of parenting issues before the baby is born, as compared to heterosexual parents—a significant proportion of whom are more or less surprised by pregnancy. Although I was already the proud stepmother of four adult children from a previous relationship, Nancy and I definitely had to plan in advance to become pregnant.

Both of us had spent a fair bit of time and energy in our younger years navigating our way through internal and external colonial divides in our own Indigenous identity development. It was very important to both of us that any child of ours would have the strongest access to kinship, culture, and land that we could build for them.

We put down our tobacco and began to look for a man who was willing to join us in this journey. We started with immediate family and then began looking farther afield. One big challenge was that there are not very many Indigenously identified sperm donors out there. We reached out to a dear friend who was also a physician and two spirited. He had already gone through the experience of fathering, both as a biological dad and stepdad. He gifted us.

Someday we may write a sitcom based on the events that took place while we were trying to get pregnant. Imagine two busy physicians living across the country from each other. Mix in some kitchen table lesbian pregnancy wisdom involving community donors. Add advice from a reproductive physiologist who knew quite a bit about both human and equine fertility, frequent air travel, and same-day courier services and you might begin to understand our simultaneously sacred, serious, and comedic attempts to co-create life and assert our Indigeneity.

After over two years of trying, we revisited our approach. We had to lie at the fertility clinic because at the time, they did not allow gay men to be sperm donors in Canada. I tried not to blush too much when I claimed to be polyamorous with a male partner who was a busy physician on the west coast and a female partner in Toronto, who was accompanying me to my appointments.

Then my auntie took me to see a healer she knew. In the sweat lodge, I was overcome with the spirit of the bear who had come into the lodge to help. For a few moments, I felt that I became that momma bear and that I was pregnant with twins—my next moon cycle I became pregnant with twins.

PREGNANT MOMMA BEAR

There are gaps in my memories of being pregnant—along with the first few sleep-deprived years of mothering twins. For the longest time after I gave birth, however, I had a strong physical recollection of my expanded belly. Today, if I try, I can still sense this powerful, uncomfortable, stretched in ways I didn't think were possible, state of being.

I remember craving bland calories and feeling nauseated. I remember a heightened, almost panicked urge, to nest with my partner. I was unreasonable in a neediness that I was not accustomed to. When she arrived home late one night with the wrong kind of toothpaste, this became clear and compelling evidence that she didn't know me and wasn't able to hear and understand my needs.

In the final months, I became anxious, as my previously sharp cognitive abilities seemed to dull. I tried to comfort myself by thinking about the significant shift in blood flow from brain to placenta that occurs in pregnancy. Hearing from friends and colleagues, whom I considered bright, that they had gone through this too helped to reassure me. They did this even when I left my car parked in downtown Toronto on Queen Street during rush hour when it was sure to get towed (and it did). I remember getting lots of love, support, and material assistance—from my partner Nancy, family, friends, work colleagues, and from my amazing team of Indigenous midwives.

BIRTH STORY

It took days for my body to go into labour. Medical technology indicated that it was time—that the boys were fully grown and ready for more space. My body and my psyche needed to "catch-up." My cervix, which had bravely and resolutely protected the sacred space of my uterus for thirty-nine years (at times against considerable odds), needed to understand it was finally safe to let go. Although I was in the medical space of the hospital, I was surrounded by strong Indigenous women and protected by a carefully prepared spirit bundle, which was pinned to the front of my blue gown.

The long-awaited labour finally took. The plan was to delay epidural pain medication until my cervix was clearly committed to fully dilating. I argued with my anesthetist, who seemed to want to ensure I was ready for an emergency Caesarean section early on in the process. However, as I progressed, my resolve became patchy. This was hard work—even for a former endurance athlete. My midwives were kind and nonjudgmental when, after a few hours, I told them I didn't know if I could keep on doing this. I hung on to my partner Nancy and my sister Diane for dear life. And made it to a delayed epidural.

We continued to work hard to balance the medical, the natural, and the spiritual within the space of the hospital. My midwives and I felt that we needed to reduce my epidural pain medication once again in the morning when I was fully dilated and ready to push out my first son, since I was quite frozen and unable to push effectively. This request was met again with some resistance by the anesthetist, who seemed to prioritize being safely ready for an emergency surgery over natural birth. And again, my own resolve wavered as I experienced the reawakening of my spinal nervous system. I amused my team by letting them know I was pretty sure that I had a pinched spinal nerve while this was happening. And then Quinn was born—caught by my long-time friend and midwife Sara.

As Quinn took his first breaths, and Nancy lifted up her shirt to suckle him, our obstetrician quickly reached inside me to find his brother Jay and break his waters. Unbeknownst to all, Jay had been doing a series of in utero acrobatics and was hung up on his umbilical cord, which had wrapped twice around his neck and once each around an arm and leg. Not a problem while he was swimming in his intact bag of waters, but now that it was ruptured, things were stressful for him. So the epidural was turned back on, and I got that emergency Caesarean section after all. I was grateful for and reliant on the expertise of the medical team in addition to the team of Indigenous family and midwives, whom I knew would protect us. Jay was born about ten minutes later. He was a little tired at first but quickly started breathing on his own steam.

In the recovery room, my midwives put both my babies on my chest, and we watched them sniff their way toward my breasts. I was physically exhausted but filled with a sense of love and family and community like nothing I had known before.

CULTURE AND RITES OF PASSAGE

Culture and its recovery can be a complex journey. For me, this story resonates with the tragic-comedic tensions of trickster or eldest brother—our fallible hero who through his antics teaches us natural law. The feelings of grief and shame at the perceived absence and loss of culture can be acute and have paralytic effects on the ability to fully imagine and actualize individual and collective identity. Yet my auntie has taught me that we often have more culture than we think we do.

My early searches for the Cree-Métis culture of my mother and grandmother were informed by notions of the great Canadian cultural mosaic. I bought into this settler-informed concept of culture as something superficial, immediately visible, and readily made available to others in the form of food, dance, and/or costume for a few hours or a day through a government grant. I mourned and felt shame at the loss of language, ceremony, song, and costume in my family. And no matter how hard I tried, I could not master the art of the jig—even when I concentrated so hard that my tongue emerged from the side of my mouth. This last sentence is supposed to be funny because part of what I have learned is the value of humour in the face of tragedy. I do look pretty funny when I try to jig.

My grandmother hid the fact that her mother tongue was Cree from me until the day she died. She knew how to fill a pantry with enough preserved food to feed a good sized family over the winter season. But when I asked her to teach me how to make our special family relish, she told me that was something I could buy from the store now.

Then I moved to Saskatchewan and spent time with Métis people—time on the land. I realized that culture was like an iceberg, and I had only been looking for the visible tip. The mountain under the water was comprised of values that had never been lost, and practices that might have been transformed were still alive and well. Along with the imprint of social justice and humility, there were strong teachings about the importance of family, self-sustenance, and sharing. These were modelled in the way that my grandmother gave up her bed and slept on the couch whenever I arrived to visit, even when she was very aged; the special family dinners that were carefully prepared and shared every Sunday when I was a child; the trips across the country to spend time with family and the way that we were welcomed during these visits; and the acreage garden kept by my auntie and uncle that had for decades supplied the local food bank.

My auntie and teacher Maria Campbell accepted our tobacco and helped us build on this base through rites of passage ceremonies for Jay and Quinn. Their Cree naming ceremony was held in Saskatoon in my friends' living room when the twins were four months old. They were laid out on a blanket in their tiny Métis sashes while our big family from all four directions gathered around. It was the first time that their paternal and maternal grandparents had met. We prayed together with the pipe. We passed them around the circle repeating their Cree names to them. Nancy and I had a big giveaway to recognize the wonderful gift we had been given and the important role that each member of the family had played in their coming to being. We feasted. We built and nourished all their relations.

Quinn took some of his first steps in his father's living room in rural British Columbia the summer just after he turned one. Jay was not far behind. That fall season, we held a walking out ceremony in the living room of our Toronto home. My auntie sewed little backpacks from Hudson Bay blankets, and as they walked around our circle of friends and family, each person put something into Quinn and Jay's backpack that symbolized a gift or skill that each friend and family member would share with the boy as he grew up. It was a powerful and beautiful ceremony. The boys still have those backpacks and love to look through the gifts they received, remembering and reinforcing their connections to each person in their ever expanding circle of kinship.

WHERE WE ARE GOING

My twins, now almost nine, believe they chose us as their family while they were stars in the skyworld and then travelled from there to be with us. Sometimes it seems overwhelming to try and raise kind Cree-Métis-Anishinaabe-Coast Salish-European settler boys in east Toronto. I worry about the way that their heads seem filled with television and videogame characters, despite my best efforts to limit screen time and expose them to Indigenous knowledge and stories. I crave more time on the land with them. Sometimes one or the other of them will say that they wish they were in a different family—one with a dad who lived in the house—or one in which they were allowed unlimited video games. But then I

- pray with and for them;
- hear their laughter in the morning;
- see them interact with the living plants and creatures in the city;
- watch them run together down the sidewalk;
- bring them with me to family and community gatherings;
- watch them interact with elders and younger cousins;
- listen to them tell others how they are very lucky because they have a very, very big family.

And then I know we are on the right path.

WHERE DO YOU COME FROM? WHO'S YOUR *NOKOMIS*?

Eneebwatung Debwewin kwe niin dizhnakawze. Rama n doonjiba. Mukwa dodem.

Greetings, my name is Nancy Cooper. I just introduced myself by my Anishinaabe name, which translated means "she who stands up for the truth and speaks from the heart." I'm from the Chippewa of Rama First Nation in southern Ontario, and I am of the Bear clan.

Often when Indigenous people are gathered, the first thing people are asked is where do they come from and then they are asked the name of their grandmother (nokomis). I love being asked that question. It tethers me to long ago; it places me in the world in a way that affirms my Indigenous identity and honours my ancestors. My nokomis's name was Nancy King, and she was a midwife. She lived into her eighties and had the softest brown skin and the thinnest white long braids.

I was born in Kapuskasing, Ontario, a pulp and paper mill town. My father, Brad, was fifth or sixth generation Irish Canadian. He'd lived in the north for some time as a gold miner but decided, for some reason, that policing was a safer career alternative. He was posted to "Kap" when I was born. I lived most of my first eighteen years living in the north—in Matheson, Moosonee, and Timmins. I consider myself a northerner with roots in southern Ontario.

In 1950 my mom, Madeleine, met and married my father within four months. They met at a dance near the reserve while my father was home in the south visiting his father. They were married in October of that year, and my mom and her young son, my eldest brother Larry, left the only life they had ever known on the reserve to venture several hundred miles north to Kirkland Lake, where my father was mining for gold. It was a hard life, with very little money left at the end of the month. But to hear them talk of those days, it was a time when they lived their lives fully and passionately. My brother Edward was born two years later.

A career change to policing and several northern towns came and went. Thirteen years passed, and I was born in 1967, their "Centennial project" they liked to joke. Growing up was tough when you are the mixed-race daughter of a white police officer and an Indigenous community worker. My mom, like a lot of Indigenous women of her generation, chose not to teach her children the Anishinaabe language or aspects of our culture, believing we would be better off the less we knew about being Indigenous. I felt bitterness as a young adult about her choices but know now, as a mother myself, the sacrifices I would make just to ensure a better life for my children than the one I have had—just like she did.

It wasn't until I went to university in Peterborough that I really started to understand what being Indigenous meant. I majored in Native studies and found my passion in community development and adult education.

Looking back, though, I see that both of my parents shared a deep, deep love of the land that they made sure was passed on to me. Every weekend, we were out in the bush, hunting, fishing, or just "poking" around, as my dad used to call it when we would drive down random bush roads south of Timmins. Without even meaning to, they were both teaching me important pieces of who I am as an Anishinaabe woman. I'll always remember the moment when my father said to me that we don't ever have to go to church because god was all around us, in every little thing. This knowledge and respect for the land has stayed with me over the years and helped to keep me centred during times of distress and the unknowing nature of life. Even today, when we are feeling stressed out as a family, we head to the bush to unwind and decompress. This is something I am so proud to share with my boys, as it tethers them to me and to their ancestors.

My mom lived long enough to meet her grandsons. "You have made me the happiest old woman alive" she wrote in a card to me. My boys won't remember their nokomis, but they will always know her name and where they come from.

GETTING READY FOR BABY

Prior to beginning my life with Janet, I had been in a long-term relationship with another woman. We skated around the idea of having a child but neither of us felt that we were ever really ready. She had a career in the theatre and travelled quite a bit, and I felt that I couldn't raise a baby on my own while she was away. So I put that idea away, locked in my heart. Then I met Janet. She was clear from the beginning that she wanted to start a family, and I realized that I could still become a mom even though I had given up on the idea.

One summer, we went on vacation with some older friends of ours. One of them is an older two-spirit Mohawk woman we really respect. We went to her to ask for advice about starting a family. I remember the sun glittering on the water and how empty the beach was that day as she grabbed a stick and started to draw on the sand. She drew images while she gave us a teaching about how we needed to spend at least two full years really learning about one another and how we were as a couple as we prepared to become parents. She talked about the importance of our roles as two mothers and our responsibility to our children to raise them as kind and loving and respectful people. I remember thinking two whole years was a long time to wait, but in the end, it was about that long before Janet got pregnant, and I realize those years were important in so many ways. Our auntie guided us well that summer long ago.

Asking our friend to donate sperm felt strange and right at the same time. Strange because I'd obviously never asked anyone for sperm before and because of him being a fairly well-known celebrity in the Indigenous community. We took tobacco and asked and all my fears melted away. He was gracious and lovely, and it felt right. Little did I know that this was the easiest part.

Over the next couple years of trying to get pregnant, there were many trips and visits and courier packages delivered to the house. Janet travelled to Vancouver, Evan travelled to Saskatoon, and donations were couriered to our place in Saskatoon. Eventually, because of work and family commitments, we moved to Toronto. We started working with a fertility clinic because trying on our own just wasn't working. We had the donations stored in Toronto and within six months, it happened. My clearest memory of that time was of watching these two teeny-weeny hearts, like two tiny universes in her body, beating in the ultrasound. After all the false starts and heartbreak, it was finally happening; we were having twins! I was terrified and excited at the same time. I remember making a joke to Janet about leaving for coffee and maybe not coming back.

There was something I hadn't done up to that point, but knew I had to finish. I had put off telling my family about the pregnancy. Although my family accepted me as a lesbian, it really wasn't something we spoke about. In many ways, I still felt very invisible to my family. Janet and I were going to have our two families together for an event so I knew that I had to tell my mom and brother first before they were blindsided by one of Janet's very excited family members. Her family was over the moon about the babies.

We went home to my mom's one weekend when I knew my brother and his wife would be there. Janet thought that making a joke about it would help make the news easier to handle. It didn't. There was a stunned silence and an awkward aftermath. Later, I was to find out that my brother demanded to know how my mother could "condone" such a thing. My mom, who was always my biggest supporter, was very quiet about the whole pregnancy. I felt her disapproval acutely. I felt invisible again. This was really hard for me to experience. To feel the joy of knowing we were going to have babies and to know I would have to do it without the support of my family was devastating.

But miracles do happen. Once my mother met her grandsons, she was in love. She was quite ill then and was on dialysis three times a week. Talking about her grandbabies, showing everyone their pictures, and providing me with all kinds of wonderful advice helped keep her spirits up. We got into a routine where after the boys were asleep in the evening, I would head outside with the phone and call her. I'd tell her about my day and all about the boys. And she would give advice or tell me stories about when her children were babies. It was a special time for me to bond with her in this way. I can still feel the summer heat and how the sky looked as I lay on the hammock under the cherry tree listening to her voice. Now we were relating as two parents, and she was able to grandparent in a way that she had never been able to before. When my oldest brother died at the age of twenty-six, his children were put up for adoption by his ex-partner. This heartbreak stayed with my mom until her death. She always wondered about her grandsons. We still do.

Perhaps the most profound thing that happened during the six months before she died was her insistence that they have a welcoming ceremony with an elder from our reserve. Auntie Hilda, who was in her late eighties at the time, came over from Rama and spent time with us for an afternoon in August when the boys were two months old. She prayed and smudged the babies, welcoming them to the family in the Anishinaabe language. Then both she and my mom officially welcomed them into the world. It was beautiful. I remember feeling so proud of my little family and even prouder still of my mom, who was, at the end of her life, able to embrace her culture and spirituality again. Mom died when the boys were only six months old. But she managed to love them enough to last them their whole lives. We talk about their nokomis all the time, and I remind the twins about who they are because of her.

The miracles continued as my brother and sister-in-law fell for the boys, too. My brother loved buying really noisy toys for them. He made them medicine pouches and beautiful leather vests for their birthday and Christmas presents. He took the time to observe their different interests. He loved their little hugs, and he really enjoyed teaching them about trucks and dogs and rabbits and plants. He died suddenly when the boys were almost seven. We miss him. My sister-in-law continues to be a constant in their lives, taking them to movies and visiting often. I am so happy to see the love in her eyes when she gets those special "auntie hugs" from the boys.

She plans to be the one to teach them to hunt when they are old enough, to take over where her husband left off. I have a theory that babies, any babies, are healing entities and spirit in bodily form. Knowing these babies, who have become boys, when there were no babies in their lives for so long, helped my family heal some part of them that was hurting.

MY WISH FOR JAY AND QUINN—AN UPBRINGING BASED ON CULTURAL CLARITY

Growing up, I didn't have a clear sense about what it meant to be Indigenous. I knew I was "Native" and that my grandmother lived on a "reserve," but beyond that, I had no real cultural conceptualization of what being Indigenous meant. I grew up white identified and dealt with being Native from an internalized racist viewpoint. I remember thinking that I wasn't like other Indigenous people. I didn't speak in a funny accent. I wore new clothes. I lived in a nice house. I was smart. I raised my hand in class: internalized racism in practice.

As I mentioned before, it wasn't until I went to university that I really started to explore my cultural identity through Native studies classes, language classes, befriending other Indigenous students, and cultural teachings provided by elders and traditional people at Trent. It was there I found a sense of self that had been missing for me. I learned about the reasons my mother lost her status when she married my father. I learned about the heartbreaking history of the treatment of my people at the hands of the church and the state. I came to understand who I was as an Anishinaabe woman. What a gift I was given during those years.

This gift is what I want my children to grow up with. It's important to me that they are provided a sense of self as Indigenous in everything we do as a family. I don't want them to grow up not knowing who they are, to feel like they don't belong anywhere, or to feel self-hatred and to internalize racism.

Both Janet and I grew up feeling like we didn't belong, without a clear sense of self. Ensuring that our boys had the right start in life was of the utmost importance to us. Janet is Cree-Métis and follows the spiritual teachings closely. We have chosen to raise Jay and Quinn this way as well. Thanks to our wonderful auntie Maria, who has so graciously and lovingly provided us with spiritual guidance and protocol, the boys have been given their traditional Cree names. Auntie Maria also guided us through the boys' walking out ceremony when they were a year old. Our family and friends gathered together in ceremony to pledge help and guidance with the raising of these boys.

The boys are also aware of their Coast Salish identity. It is very important that they spend time with their wonderful family from the Sliammon First Nation, which is Evan's home community. His whole family has welcomed the boys, Janet, and me into their family. We have committed to spending part of each summer there so that the boys can grow up knowing this large extended family. Evan's parents Leslie and Jeannie are wonderful people who have taught us so much about the importance of love and family responsibility. On the reserve, the boys spend time with their cousins and blend right in—right where they belong. They are registered band members in Sliammon. This was a decision we made early on because Evan has the stronger connection with his home community. Because of the archaic Indian Act, my mother was no longer considered a band member when she married my father. Although we did regain our status in 1985, her link to community was beyond repair and as a result, I've never had a strong connection to Rama.

The Sliammon people have just recently celebrated the implementation of their treaty with the federal government and are no longer governed by the Indian Act. I'm proud to know my children are part of this historic time for the Sliammon people and will grow up only knowing a self-determining home community.

NONBIOLOGICAL MOM—WHAT IT HAS MEANT TO ME

When we made the decision that Janet would get pregnant, I wondered how and where I would fit into the role of mother. Would the babies feel like they were my sons? I needn't have worried. It has been the most natural thing in the world for me to mother these boys. They were mine the second I saw those tiny beating hearts on the ultrasound.

I tried to breastfeed with the help of some medication and a lot of pumping in the weeks prior to the babies being born. Basically, I tricked my body into thinking it was pregnant. I did manage to produce some milk but not enough for any long-term feeding. When Quinn was born, I was able to get him to latch immediately. What a special time the two of us had while Jay was being born. We stared at each other, and I formally introduced myself. We were skin to skin, and he nosed his way to my breast. Later, Janet would take on the huge task of feeding the boys, but for that short time, I was able to provide some sustenance to my baby boy. My advice to anyone who isn't a birth mother wanting to breastfeed is to start early and be willing to pump every couple of hours for weeks leading up to the birth. I wasn't able to maintain this type of schedule because by the end of her pregnancy, Janet needed a lot of extra care.

I was worried about how we would be perceived by others—two women having babies together. I worried about what people would say and how the boys would be treated. I guess living in Toronto, a very liberal city, has helped, but it really has been a nonissue for our little family. I never felt the need to educate other people about the makeup of our family. Oh sure I would answer people if they asked about who carried the babies, but it hasn't been as important to me as I thought it would be. We just are another version of what a family looks like. In fact on our street in Toronto, there are least three lesbian couples with kids, and so far, the boys have not been faced with difficult questions about their moms.

We are both accepted as the parents of the boys in our community. I have taken on a larger part of the caregiving and housekeeping role in the family. I work part time, and I am currently able to drop the boys off at school and pick them up. I legally adopted the boys when they were born. We are both identified as parents on the boys' birth certificates. I've travelled with them on my own across borders and have only been questioned once by a rude border agent. But we both travel with adoption papers and a letter outlining our legal family makeup. As a queer family, we almost expect to get hassled at borders, but even this is less and less a worry as the years go by.

IMPORTANCE OF COMMUNITY

It is crucial for me to try to convey how important community has been for me while raising these young boys. The love and support of our friends and neighbours has been overwhelming. From the day they were born, we have been blessed with a loving and thoughtful community of people who support us on this journey. The boys have many nonbiological aunties and uncles who they rely on for guidance and teachings. They have several older nonbiological cousins who care for them on a regular basis. Our neighbours have an open-door policy and the boys go over and walk right in if they want to have a visit. Our male friends are important role models for the boys as well. Jay and Quinn are growing up learning about being kind men with the help of our wonderful friends. I cherish these gifts in all of their various forms. I love that my family is in a constant state of becoming:

becoming closer;
becoming wiser;
becoming more loving;
becoming whole.

ENDNOTE

[1]Road allowance is land reserved by government for public roads. After multiple forced dislocations from traditional lands, many Métis on the prairies set up communities on road allowances and railway reserve lands and became known as "Road Allowance People." In Saskatchewan, commencing in the 1940s, as part of the farming rehabilitation policy, Métis were forced by the provincial government to leave their road allowance homes and communities—once again dislocated from their homeland.

5.
Sacred Voice Woman's Journey as an Indigenous Auntie

PAULETE POITRAS

THERE ARE MOMENTS in your life that mark a before and an after. Before I became an auntie, I thought I knew it all. You know that age when you think the world owes you something. I was eighteen when I thought I knew it all. I had this sense of entitlement and my ignorance of what the world was like was undeniably annoying. In reflection, I was green to how the world was. I had an obsessive, compulsive mother who believed in old-fashioned discipline. She groomed me not to question anything and gave me a high tolerance to pain. I was fresh off the reserve. My lack of knowledge and common sense was pitiful, and marked me as ignorant. I definitely had no clue. But one thing I was sure of was that I knew where I belonged. I had pride, confidence, ignorance, and resiliency—a Dakota Cree with the moral fiber of old-school beliefs and the knowledge of my ancestors coursing through my veins. I took that bus to Vermillion, Alberta, with anticipation and happiness knowing I was going to be an auntie. Unsure of the life lessons that lied ahead, I got on that bus, and my life has never been the same since.

TURNING POINT

I had never lived far from my parents before, but I was eighteen and legally an adult. I didn't know much, but I was so happy for change in my life. My entire life existence was sheltered right up until that point. My older sister Amber met this young man from Goodfish Lake First Nations, and they were expecting their first child. Being an auntie was going to be the most important role in my life. I rode the bus from Regina to Saskatoon and then changed buses in Saskatoon to journey to Vermillion, close to where my sister lived. My sister and I planned ahead of time for her to be waiting for me on the other end. The bus ride was long, and I ended up having a long conversation with three people on the bus. I distinctly remember thinking "Wow I have so much confidence to be talking to complete strangers and actually connecting with them." Looking back, I trusted too much and made myself vulnerable to any dangers that might have lied ahead.

A SISTER'S LOVE

Being the youngest of two had both its benefits and disadvantages. My sister Amber and I are four years apart, and she always looked out for me. Despite our age difference, we were close growing up. Our parents always raised us to be responsible for each other and ourselves. I love my sister; she is my first best friend. Amber taught me about sacrifice, as she sacrificed a lot by looking after me. Amber braided my hair, fed me, and did her best to ensure that nobody hurt me. So when Amber became pregnant, it was such a blessing, and I wanted to be there when the baby was born so I could thank her for all that she had sacrificed for me. I asked her if I could come help her with the baby and with excitement, we planned for me to stay with her.

As the Greyhound came rolling into the tiny little town, I saw a gas station and a blue car; there was my round-bellied sister waving at me. I remember being so happy, and all I wanted to do was kiss her belly. I gave her a big hug, grabbed my bag, and got in the car. My sister was sitting in the passenger side just smiling hard, when she looked back at me and asked how the ride was. I replied, "It was long, but I'm glad I'm here." With her boyfriend driving, we continued on and stopped in St. Paul for a late supper at some fast-food place. After we ate, we went to their place. I remember thinking what a small apartment they had with such few things, but they had each other with this blessing on the way and that's all that really mattered. I slept on the couch after a long visit with my sister and her boyfriend. I was feeling unsure and a bit afraid of being there. I was uncertain what lied ahead, but I figured the next day I'd go to my sister's work and print off some résumés to find employment.

MY EARLIER YEARS

Even though I was the youngest, I wasn't allowed to be lazy. I was taught that with hard work, respect, and discipline, one could attain any form of success. When I was younger, I was known for wandering around with my dog always doing something. I remember walking for hours with adventure on my mind. However, I knew that before I left for any adventure, I had to complete my chores. I had responsibilities, and doing chores was one of them. My chores included cleaning the house, doing yard work, tending the garden, and taking care of my animals. I always completed all my chores and responsibilities before I had any time to play. It was then when I developed pride in my work.

When I was younger, I was constantly busy helping our neighbours, my grandfather, and his brother. They always kept me busy with weeding the garden, cleaning yard, and cutting wood. As a collective, they taught me the sweet joys of independence and the payoff of hard work. They knew that I wasn't lazy but rather a reliable person. If I committed myself to doing something or helping someone, I always fulfilled my commitments. I was fortunate to have these elders in my life grooming me to be a resilient and successful person. I am thankful for both mushum (grandfather) Calvin and mushum Noel Junior, who blessed my life with their guidance. A healthy understanding of roles and responsibilities of my place within the family helped me create a positive transformation of character.

The very next morning I woke up to my sister cooking breakfast and asking me to get ready as I was accompanying her to work. After we ate breakfast, we drove to her work at the Native Friendship Centre in St. Paul. She was a coordinator of some sort—I can't really recall what her position was, but she helped youth in the community and that was important. I was introduced to her co-workers, and some of them were our Poitras relatives from Kehiwin First Nation. I only remembered them from the family reunions of the years past. Afterwards, I went to my sister's office and printed off copies of my résumé. During her lunch hour, I handed out my résumé to different places. I came across this employment centre, where I filled out an application and gave them a copy of my résumé. I felt excited about this new place and that I was an adult now. It seems funny to me now to think just how naïve I was.

A week went by, and I had probably cleaned my sister's apartment a dozen times. I finally got a call back from a local restaurant asking if I could come in for an interview. Excited, I let my sister know. I made a call to my parents, and my mom picked up. I let her know the good news, and she was satisfied with my new job offer. My dad got on the phone and prepared me for the interview and gave me tips on how to dress for it. My dad was always supportive toward me that way.

DADDY'S GIRL

Growing up, I was always close with my dad. I spent most of my time with him and following him around. I remember looking up to him, my role model, and I just wanted to be exactly like him. I saw him as a direct, honest, respectful, and caring dad. He was good to my sister and me. We knew it too. We knew we could somehow convince him of our plans, and sooner than later, he would agree to them. With my dad as my role model, I began to take on roles of a strong Dakota male. Although I was not a male, it did not stop me from learning from my dad. I spent endless hours learning things he taught me. He taught me how to cook, shine my cowboy boots, iron a shirt, tie a tie, ride a horse, saddle a horse, dance pow wow, throw a football, play fastball, read a measuring tape, braid my hair, understand politics, understand Indigenous history, cut wood, pray, respect ceremony, and, most importantly, love. His favorite saying was "Thatta boy my girl," when he was proud of my achievements.

I walked back from my interview confident and proud of myself. I felt as though I had answered every question well. When I got back to the apartment, I phoned home. My mom answered, and she was happy to hear that I did well. She gave me brief highlights of the reserve life I left behind. She let me know my mushum came by asking about me. She assured him that I was doing well and had an interview. He told her "That's good, that's really good. You know that kid has the smarts and a good work ethic; she'll get the job." She told me next time he was over that she would call me so I could talk to him. I thanked her and hung up. I was so happy and wished that one day my mom would say that she was proud of me or better yet that she loved me.

A MOTHER'S LOVE

The most important part of growing up was being taught at a young age to work hard. Nothing in life is free. My mother saw the importance of hard work and determination. She was our disciplinary parent. She didn't allow disrespect or back talk: she taught us to be honest and proud Indigenous young women. The role of balancing all aspects of life was difficult. Although she was strict, she taught us about respect. She didn't always say she loved us, but she taught us the quiet ways of showing affection, such as making soup and bannock after being apart from a loved one. She always ensured that there was food on the table and that I had a safe place to sleep and clean clothes to wear. I know that these things are thought to be freely given as a parent, but I am forever thankful for her sacrifices. She made sure that we knew the importance of family and prayer. "A family that prays together stays together" was her saying.

The very next day I woke up early and got ready for the day. I just was finishing eating when the phone rang. I quickly answered the phone, and it was a man from the local restaurant offering me a job as a waitress. He asked if I was available today to meet, do paperwork, and get my shift schedule. I let him know that I accepted the offer and was available today. He said to meet him at eleven at the back of the restaurant. So I walked there excited and filled with anticipation. It was my first job as an adult. I was proud and confident of this new opportunity. I got there early—a whole half hour early. Eager to work, I waited.

My new boss drove up to the restaurant up to the door in his new car. I got a quick tour of the restaurant as he went over rules, responsibilities; I also got a uniform, a *POSiTouch* card, and shift schedule. I left happy knowing I was going to try out waitressing. It was a good change. I didn't know what to expect, but I looked forward to the whole experience.

Reflections provide insight to my character and assist in the development of my moral compass. I see when I look back into my past that I had ambition, hope, happiness, and confidence. I admire that person I once was. I do not have any regrets of the life I have led thus far, but I see now that it was pride that got me in the most trouble. Not the pride I grew up with, but with the kind that protected my ego.

MY MENTOR, MY MUSHUM

The pride that I had before was a healthy sense of self. It was developed through the support and guidance of a mentor. Although I am both Dakota and Cree, I gravitated closer to my Dakota culture because my mushum Calvin lived so close to us. My other grandparents who were Cree lived in Kawakatoose First Nation, and we resided on Muscowpetung First Nation. Although I did spend time with my Cree grandparents I had constant communication with my grandfather Calvin, my dad's dad. My mushum Calvin was a fluent Dakota speaker, and as a young girl, I was taught by him how to speak in Dakota. Unfortunately I did not keep my fluency, but when I am around fluent speakers, my memories and comprehension comes flooding back. He assisted in raising my older sister and me. He lived just across the road from us and always came over for a visit. We would make him coffee and offer him any sweets we might have had around. He would just talk small talk about the weather, what's new on the reserve, and he would always ask about how we were doing in school. On special occasions, my mushum would come just to share old stories; this was a great treat, and we cherished these talks.

Throughout my life, I always reflect on his visits. It was a daily event, but we were always taught to speak to our grandfather with respect. We never realized, however, that his visits and stories gave knowledge and teachings. He told us of our bloodline, where we came from, and how we ended up in Muscowpetung. He told us of other families and their history as he was knowledgeable in these things and he was our very own library. When he passed away, we thought that we had lost everything, but we came to realize that because of those stories, we remember the teachings, and even in death, he remains our library.

ORAL HISTORY

Oral history is an Indigenous method of teaching life lessons. I was raised "old school," with oral teachings from my greatest mentor, my mushum Calvin Poitras. He told me stories that were passed down to him when he was just a young boy from his grandfather and so forth. He always said "Never add to or take away from the teachings but keep the teachings simple as possible." This was set in place to keep intact the morals and ethics of Dakota culture. My mushum once told me a great story, which I hold close whenever I pursue something new in life.

You know all of us here on Earth have purpose. Put your right hand as though you are pinching something and push it towards your left side of your chest. Put your right hand over your heart and push into your chest. This is so that you will know that with a good heart and good intentions, everything will work out in a good way. The heartbeat that you have is called purpose. Take time to give thanks for those who died before you. You have a long rich history of ancestors before you. They died with purpose, they lived each day as a blessing, and they fought with your intentions to live life as a good person. In turn, it's up to you to live for others.

Everyone wants to be the seventh generation. The seventh is the generation of hope and inspiration. In reality, every person is already the seventh generation of the seven before. It is your job to think of those seven generations after you (Acoose 117-118). You need to build a solid foundation for those after you and maintain those teachings before you. Know who you are, and you will always know where you are going. You will sometimes feel lost and forget who you are. Put your right hand as though you are pinching something and push it toward the left side of your chest. Above your heart, know and remind yourself from time to time that you have purpose. Teach this to everyone you know.

Make these words contagious and pass them along to everyone you know. People will hear you, and you will be like a rock that has been thrown into water that causes a ripple. It will lift those who need it and inspire those who hear it. "*Chântê wâstê*" means "good heart" in Dakota. You are good medicine. The histories of our ancestors are Indigenous-inherited rights to self-awareness and a link to a healthy understanding of self.

On my long walk back from the restaurant to the apartment, I remembered my mushum's words, and I pinched my fingers together on my right hand. I pushed my hand into the left side of my chest. I whispered "*Chântê wâstê*" to myself. Just after a few minutes of being home, I was looking at my new uniform and the phone rang. I answered it, and it was my mom. She said someone here wants to talk to you. Then this loud husky voice yelled, "HELLO MISS POLLY. HOW ARE YOU?" I replied, "Hi mushum. I'm good, and how are you?" My mushum Calvin yelled into the phone, "I'M GOOD! I'M REALLY GOOD, IT'S GETTING COLDER, COLD OUT TODAY WITH THAT WIND, BUT I'M REALLY GOOD. I HEARD YOU GOT A JOB OFFER. HOW DID THAT GO?" He only yelled because he couldn't hear properly. I said, "Yup, I got my uniform, signed papers, and got a work schedule today, mushum." "THAT'S GOOD. THAT'S REALLY GOOD. I'M REALLY PROUD OF YOU." "Thanks mushum. Love you mushum, and I miss you lots!" "THAT'S GOOD. I MISS YOU TOO. I ALWAYS PRAY FOR YOU EVERYDAY, THREE TIMES A DAY!" "Thanks mushum. I pray for you too! I love you mushum." "YA, OK YOU TOO. *TOKSÂ ÂKÊ*." My mushum struggled with telling me he loved me, but I knew he loved me. I felt it, right there in my heart. I knew I was lucky to have him as a part of my life. He always guided me throughout my life, and he always reminded me that I made the right choice when I chose him as my grandfather.

CREATION STORY

Spiritual awareness has nothing to do with fact or fiction; it is a measure of one's faith. The one story that I commonly share is the Creation story of how everyone transitions from spirit to our physical existence. My mushum Calvin told me the following:

> Before we come here to live here on Grandmother Earth, we were all this round ball of light and energy. We sat with the Creator of life and made an agreement with the Creator. Our agreement consisted of who we are, who our parents would be, what bloodline we would come from, the details of trials and tribulations of life, our purpose, our promises of how we would live, our mistakes, our successes, what the children would or would not have, the love we would experience, the lessons we would learn, the day we would begin our journey of life, the day we would end our journey of life and, most importantly, our contribution to our people. We would make this promise to the Creator, and then we would come to the agreement. However, with our first cry when we are born into this world, we forget our agreement. We are brought into this world forgetting, but as we go through life, we relearn our agreement. We are all born with a gift, each unique nothing the same, possibly similar but never the same. This gift we were each given was a gift to share to help each other and, most importantly, help ourselves. Nobody can own us—not our own parents, our own family, our own culture, not even our own selves. Our souls were borrowed from the Creator of life. Our own life was the greatest gift and blessing given to each of us. No one is built better than the next.

This particular story became my philosophy of my life, and the older I have grown, the more I have come to understand it.

I was a few weeks into working as a waitress, and I really enjoyed it. One evening a co-worker invited me to their small gathering at their place after work. I accepted without any notion that this would be the evening my sister would go into labour and my days of being an auntie would start.

HUMBLE BEGINNINGS

Life's lessons help shape the character of a personal moral compass and the growth of ethical perspectives. It was my first night going out in a new town, and I was at this house party with co-workers. The phone rang after a couple hours of being there. A person answered the call and asked the group, "Is there a Paulete here?" I turned around to look in their direction and said, "Yeah, that's me." I got up to answer the phone, and to my surprise, I heard a familiar voice; it was my sister. "Where are you? I've been trying to find you. Hurry up and get home! I'm going into labour." Bang, she hung up. How did she find me? I asked if anyone wanted to drive my vehicle to my sister's place. A co-worker of mine replied, "Sure I'll go with you. I haven't been drinking." It was a sigh of relief on my end; I had drunk too much to drive.

We quickly put our jackets on, slipped on our shoes, and said our goodbyes. We walked downstairs to go outside, and a brisk breeze hit us. I gasped, and suddenly I started to feel a bit more intoxicated. I pointed to my vehicle—an old dodge burgundy van with a painted wolf's mural on the sides of it—and we walked toward it and got in. It fired right up, and I directed us to my place. Then she asked me, "So what's the big hurry?" I looked at her a bit stunned and intoxicated. I let the question hit the forefront of my mind and then said "It's my sister. She's in labour. I'm the only one with a vehicle, and she probably needs it to get to the hospital. It's her first baby." All I could think was of all the damn nights to go out and drink, why tonight? I shook my head at my poor decision. We arrived at the apartment, and I thanked my co-worker for the ride. Then she gave me the keys. We got out and walked in opposite direction. I moved toward the main doors to our apartment building.

I walked down the stairs into the building. I tried to put my keys in the door, and the door quickly opened. A highly excited and nervous face greeted me; it was my sister's boyfriend, Cody, who was quickly followed from behind by the very annoyed and anxious face of Amber, her face contorted by both labour and disapproval. She grabbed the keys out of my hand and waddled out of the apartment while Cody moved ahead of her, with a bag in his hand. She yelled at him, "Cody! Wait for me!" He stopped, turned around, and grabbed her by her hand as they walked up the stairs.

I was standing there, with no excuse to give. Feeling a bit ashamed for being intoxicated, I took the extra house keys left on the kitchen table. I walked out of the apartment, and I locked the door behind me. I walked a few blocks from the apartment toward the hospital.

At the hospital, I asked at the reception desk where my sister was. Given directions, I walked in the direction that the nurse gave me. I get to the room, and there was the annoyed face of my labouring sister. She started scolding me for going out and not letting her know where I was. Cody walked in the room, smiling, but when he saw her scolding me, he turned around and walked out. I stood there with my head down, trying to gather any form of verbal defense but nothing came. I just stared at the floor thinking, "Holy shit. I didn't do this intentionally."

A couple hours went by, and her pain increased. The alcohol still lingered in my body, and I sipped on burnt coffee, hoping to sober up a little. Odd thoughts ran through my mind, and I looked at my sister, who was still annoyed with me. The doctor came in to check her and said, "Well, it looks like that time." Cody held my sister's hand and did everything he could to comfort her. She glared at me and said in a stern voice, "I want you in there with me but don't do anything stupid." I nodded my head with confirmation, and they wheeled her in the direction of the delivery room.

They told Cody and me to wash our hands. We then proceeded to put on a mask, gown, and gloves. Cody was filled with a mixture of anxiety and excitement. I, on the other hand, just went through the motions, unsure what to feel. Thoughts of, "Wow, this is it. I'm going to be an auntie" settled in. I stood on the right side of my sister's bed, with Cody on the left side. She settled into position to start to deliver. The nurses assisted her, and the doctor came in with a young woman at his side. He told us that she is an intern doctor and asked if she could do the procedure. Too filled with pain to disagree, Amber just nodded her head.

The pain increased, and Cody and the nurse told her to push. Feeling a bit intoxicated, I spoke out of sync with them, and my sister, flushed red with the first push, glared at me. Not thinking, I said to her, "Holy, your face is as red as a tomato." She stared at me and yelled, "SHUT UP and just stand there!" The doctor nodded at the nurse assisting, and she said, "Okay, Amber time to push again." She pushed while both Cody and the nurse cheered her on. Standing there with nothing to say, I watched everything go on, and halfway through pushing, the doctor asked her, "The baby is crowning. Do you want to feel?" Almost disgusted, she screamed "NO!" I leaned over to look, and it was an image that promised years of birth control. My body filled with sympathy pains, and I looked at my sister with pride. She continued to push again, and the baby came out. Except that the doctor and his stupid intern had their backs turned. I was so angry because the baby hit the table first. Pissed off, I said, "What the hell, the baby hit the table!" The doctor quickly picked up the baby, ignored me, and pretended that he had caught the baby in time, and said to Amber and Cody, "Your baby is here!" We were all crying when Cody was given the scissors to cut the umbilical cord. They took the baby to weigh him and a tiny little cry came out and then again. He was scared of the sound of his own crying, and we all laughed. A sigh of relief came from my sister, and Cody walked over to comfort her. He walked over to the baby, smiled, and I shook his hand, saying, "Congratulations bro, you're a dad." He smiled again, and my sister told me to move out of the way so that she could see the baby. I moved, and she was crying. I went over and kissed her on the forehead, whispering, "You're a mommy now! I'm happy for you." She beamed but was still annoyed with me, yet her anger slowly subsided with the baby in the room. Cody rushed over to Amber to kiss and love her up, and just like that, they were a family.

Just as I glanced over at the baby, I saw those little brown eyes looking up at me: this new curious wonder was staring at me and I began to cry. I was overwhelmed with happiness but was a little disappointment in myself. I whispered to the baby, "Hi baby, I'm your auntie Paulie. I'm sorry for not being in the right frame of mind right now, but I couldn't miss your birth for the world. I love you, and yet I just met you. This is what they meant when they said love at first sight. I get it now. Thank you for choosing us and being here, healthy and happy." I gently touched his tiny little cheek with my hand, as I was fearful of kissing him with alcohol on my breath. It was that moment in my life that changed my whole worldview. I stayed for about an hour afterwards and headed back home to the apartment where I fell asleep. Each story has a humble beginning, and each story continues on with each chapter of personal growth.

Being an Indigenous auntie helps me realize just how differently our roles are within society in modern times. With time, growth happens along with maturity. I have struggled with abusive relationships, addiction, and trauma. I feel as though life is a journey and through it all, we are to preserve, protect, and sustain our identity as Indigenous people. Being an auntie is like being a second mother. It is an honour, and we need to always give thanks to our siblings for that gift of life.

GRATITUDE FOR MY RELATIONSHIPS

Now that we are grown up, my sister and I have different perspectives, opinions, views, and understandings in life. I respect the fact that we are not the same. But we do have the same humble beginnings. Although Amber is older, I feel protective of her. The older I get, the more protective I become of her. I have Amber's best intentions in mind as I provide the best advice I can. No matter the distance or the circumstance, I will always be there for my sister. I will always support her and love her endlessly. I am forever grateful for everything Amber has done for me. Thank you sister for always bringing laughter and sharing those young memories with me, I honestly wouldn't change a thing. I love you, and I always will respect you Amber. Thank you sister for bringing these tiny lives into my life and changing me for the better.

I wasn't that close to my mother growing up, but now I consider her one of my best friends. She has taught me to speak my mind, to voice my opinions, and has encouraged me to attain my education. She is my rock, and I love her so much. I knew at a young age that I couldn't get away with much, but I appreciate her strict ways because she taught me many great lessons. She kept me out of harm's way and did the best that she could with what she had. I talk to her almost every day, and we have a healthy relationship. Our humour has grown, and we can just have a wonderful conversation. She respects, accepts, and supports the healthy lifestyle that I live and for that, I am forever grateful to have chosen her as my mother in this life. Thanks mommy Marcie; I love and respect you always.

As the years passed and I grew into a woman, my relationship with father grew too. For ten years, my dad has been battling type 2 diabetes and within those years, his health has deteriorated. Through my adult life, I have been a major support for my dad. I'm always there for him when he needs me, and I do my best to keep my family calm when it comes to his health. He is on dialysis three times a week and has lost his vision due to glaucoma. I realize now that I am older how our roles have reversed, and I am now taking care of him. My parents reside in Muscowpetung, and I go back home to cut my dad's hair and shave his face. He really enjoys these moments together. We laugh and tell stories to each other. It's a great time to reconnect as father and daughter. I truly love him, and I am honoured to have him in my life. I often take time to thank him for all his teachings. I always tell him I love him. Thanks Daddy Dutto for your endless love and support throughout my life journey. I love you so much. You will always be number one, and I will always "love you thirty-five bucks." The story behind the thirty-five bucks is that when I was young, that was the most money I had ever had. He once asked me, "how much do you love me?" and I replied, "thirty-five bucks."

In these modern times, I give thanks for those old teachings. They guide me through all the turmoil, trials, and tribulations. I only strive to be a better person than I was the day before. I acknowledge that the ones that call me auntie look up to me as their role model. So I try my best to model a healthy lifestyle. Kinship is important, and preserving those bonds works toward creating a positive community.

KINSHIP AND ADOPTING OF RELATIONS

As I grew older and attended school, I gained friendships outside my family circle. Some of those friendships lasted just through my schooling year, but others became an extension of my family circle. I have gained respect from those close bonds and have respected these relations as blood relatives. Despite not sharing the same bloodline, I called these friends my brothers and sisters, and these friendships turned into the most sincere and respectful relationships. In my culture, this is called "adopting of relations," and I call them my adopted family.

Being adopted into families or adopting someone into your family is one of the highest honours attained in life. To be adopted is respecting that kinship as though it is your flesh and blood. An adoption of a relative may happen in order to fill the void of a lost loved one or to increase respectful boundaries between friendships. Through my adopted relatives, I inherit their children as my nieces and nephews, and accrue the responsibility of being their auntie. I am fortunate to have lots of adopted relatives—nieces, nephews, siblings, parents, grandparents, families—and I am beyond grateful to be a part of all my families. I hold my responsibilities intact and honourably.

My adopted relatives are from all over. I've been adopted into many different families from many different tribes. Everywhere I go, I have a home and a place to stay. I love my entire family, extended family, and adopted relatives. Kinship is important to the growth and maturity of self. Family is the biggest support system through all stages of life. It forgives quickly and supplies endless love.

I have relied a lot on mentoring from my mushum Calvin. He has always given me good honest advice. He has allowed me to make mistakes, and he asks that I reflect on the choices I have made. There is always room for growth, maturity, love, understanding, and life lessons in his teachings, and these values have helped me continue to develop my own will power. He always said, "Creator gave us many gifts and one of them is willpower. You may have spoken to the Creator about your life purposes, lessons, and major life choices, but he gave all of us the opportunity to choose our moments of readiness. When you are ready, you make better choices. Time does that for all of us."

WHAT DOES "COMMUNITY RAISED" MEAN?

I take pride in my role of being an auntie. My auntie duties are not reserved only for my sister's children. I was raised with the theory of "community raising," which says that raising a child is not just the responsibility of the parents but of everyone within the community. People of Indigenous cultures often rely on extended family to contribute to childrearing.

Family structure generally consists of two types: the nuclear family structure, and the alternative family structures. The nuclear family is a (heterosexual) couple and their dependent children, regarded as a basic (normative) social unit. Alternative family forms—such as same sex relationships, single parent households, and adopting individuals—are more common. I was raised in a nuclear family. My family often brought other family members from outside our nuclear structure, which transitioned us into an alternative family structure. For example, in my own upbringing, my first cousins came to live with my family. I was raised to understand that my first cousins were to be treated with the same respect as my siblings. Calling my male cousins my brothers and female cousins my sisters was considered respectful.

From growing up on the reserve my whole life, the majority of my friendships, and close bonds, were with my first cousins. Therefore, it was normal that I called my cousins my brothers and sisters. It only became confusing when explaining to people outside our family. We usually smiled and simply said, "Yeah, that's my older brother, can't you tell?" I wanted the message to be clear: I respect my relations. Respectful connections with self, kinship, and community is a way to connecting to life's purpose.

PURPOSE

The purpose in being an Indigenous auntie is to pass the knowledge that was given to me into everyday activities. When I am approached by any niece or nephew about things they need or want, I often weigh out what is actually needed or wanted. I approach all their scenarios with love and understanding. Just like them, I had limited resources and support, so I try to give them honest answers that will go alongside the teachings of their parents. For example, I often get questions of a spiritual nature. I have an adopted niece, and she was really stressed out over her hockey. She needed to balance her physical training with having a part-time job. I made small talk, asked about her hockey, asked about her training, asked how work was going, and then she started to open up. She made a bold statement: "Sometimes my friends don't understand me, or my parents, maybe it's me?!? I don't know." I told her:

> You are different than the rest. You have spiritual gifts that nobody acknowledges nor understands, and pressures to achieve your goals. You are a young, strong, resilient Indigenous woman, and while you will always be different, you need to celebrate that fact. Your parents love you, and you need to celebrate that fact also. Not everyone has these privileges. There are many generations before you who fought and died for freedom that you take for granted. Honour them the best way you can, honour your differences from your friends and take time to thank your parents for the sacrifices they make so you can have the privileges you have. You are young and talented. You have abilities that come so easy to you, and that alone is something to honour. I remember growing up, I had to do things differently. I often prayed to be "normal": like the rest of my peers. I know now that I choose this life. I am proud to be a Dakota Cree and full of ancestral knowledge and rich history that openly celebrates our spirituality. Not everyone has the gift to celebrate, but the key is balance.

She smiled after I answered her questions and thanked me with a big hug. She wasn't alone in her worries and for her to know she had this spiritual support meant anything was possible.

I have many adopted nieces and nephews. My role as their auntie grows and develops over time. I hold a unique bond with each of them. I often have to find a balance, as I play dual roles of being an Indigenous auntie in modern times and teaching Indigenous ancestral knowledge. The greatest gift so far in life for me has been sharing and providing guidance to those younger than me. I lead a happy, healthy, and sober lifestyle. My life isn't about fame or fortune but of humble blessings. I am grateful for all that I have. I often spend my time sewing, beading, supporting the community, participating in ceremony, and working. I make time for any niece or nephew who asks for any form of guidance or supportive words, and trusted with their ideas, worries, issues, life lessons, success, failures, happiness, goals, and day-to-day activities is a blessing all its own. Although I am human and sometimes may have moments of weakness or poor judgment, I forgive quickly and take accountability first. My purpose and main goal is to give honest simple advice. I wasn't lied to when it came to my mushum. He taught me about honesty and understanding. I try my best to maintain honesty and fulfill the role of an Indigenous auntie.

MY MUSHUM CALVIN TAUGHT ME TO CELEBRATE MY DIFFERENCES

My mushum Calvin gave me responsibilities to work hard, and he always had a task at hand for me. Little did I know at the time that he was giving me male roles, and he always knew even then that I was two spirited. He would tell me of the *winkte* society, the two-spirited clan:

> Creator knows what he is doing even when he makes our people with two spirits. Creator does not make mistakes; he is our Creator, and he gives of life through the female. Respect his decisions. The two spirits are our teachers, and we are not meant to shame them but learn from them. Because they come from a society, they have gifts of their own. Most similar to one another, their abilities come from both male and female roles. They have a duty to be messengers from this world to the spirit world. Know and understand that you have these abilities.

I didn't know at the time, but he was giving me my blessing to be my most authentic self. I love that he loved me for who I was and never tried to push me away. My mushum always believed in respect for women's rights (Green 21). Thank you mushum for your unconditional love. Confidence comes when love, support, and understanding was given to me by my mentor.

INDIGENOUS COMMUNITY RESPONSIBILITIES

Indigenous people believe they have a responsibility for all members of the community who have a place and need to teach in the community. I openly speak to all youth from all walks of life, not just my relatives or adopted relatives. I have the ability to engage youth. I share the knowledge given to me, and, therefore, I do my part in "community raising." I actively build communication with youth everywhere I go. Regardless of the circumstances that any child or youth speak to me about, I see each of their unique potentials. With just a few words of advice and wisdom, I encourage them to push towards a more positive lifestyle.

I was fortunate enough to have a mentor such as my mushum Calvin, but not everyone is as fortunate enough to have a supportive person who listens. So I take each opportunity to listen to our youth. They are our future, and one day I may depend on those youth to care for me. To my mind, an investment in any youth is an investment in caregiving to seven generations thereafter.

APPROACHING ANSWERS THROUGH HUMOUR

Humour is common in any Indigenous culture. We use humour to tell stories, share ideas, scold, and heal. Often humour is used for the mere pleasure of sharing laughter and spreading joy. Indigenous people use humour to heal and often reflect on what the journey has taught us. It is used as a tool to tell stories, share, and gather community. As an auntie, I use humour as a tool to help teach lessons of life to those who seek guidance. This way is easily adopted and helps to ease the tension that can arise from more serious circumstances. Although what I talk about is taken seriously, the lesson is taught through laughter and self-actualization. The information stays with the person and comes to life all on its own. Our stories use humour to help make them memorable.

DISCIPLINE

Although at this time in my life I do not yet have children of my own, being someone's auntie has always been my greatest role in life. I'm a daughter, a granddaughter, a sister, a partner, a friend, but being someone's auntie brings a different aspect and fun into my life. I am the person that youth turn to for advice, conversations, fun, and laughter. The majority of the time it's fun, but I also have the responsibility to keep them in line. Discipline does not need to be physically, emotionally, mentally, or spiritually abusive. Discipline is used to teach the youth to understand the consequences of their actions. With just words and a change in tone, their attitude is put in check, and they are held accountable for their behaviour. I balance my roles as the disciplinarian and the fun auntie at all times. My nieces and nephews know that they can tell me anything. They know that I am always available to speak to about how they feel and to express their efforts to deal with the issues that they face. I maintain and regulate their safety, and often remind them of the ethics, morals, and expectations of their parents when they make their choices. As we all know, our path is ours to make, and, therefore, our own lessons are ours to make as well. There is no harm done sharing stories with our young ones. These lessons are our teachers, and it may save someone from enduring a hardship. Sharing knowledge is key to being a good auntie.

STRUGGLES

Oftentimes, we take for granted the time we share with those we love. Family gatherings allow significant time with each other, and in those moments, you get the opportunities to share, teach, and laugh. Oftentimes, we gather at times of loss. Death is a part of life, and it is life's greatest teacher. Although death is hard, it teaches us about the past and future.

When a person dies at a young age, the grief is unbearable, as that once bright life is now gone. It hurts not just the family but the entire community. I sadly lost one of my nephews at birth, as he was stillborn. This was hard on the family knowing a little life was taken too soon. Warren Calvin Memnook "*wâyinâh kâcî yâkâ*" (Sit with Thunder) was born into the spirit world on 22 January 2008 at 10:15 a.m. At just thirty-five weeks, he was three pounds and four ounces. I never felt so heartbroken and helpless in my life. My heart was so heavy that I felt as though I couldn't breathe. My sister was falling apart. I had to maintain my place as a sister and balance my role as an auntie. It was hard to overcome, but through prayer, support, therapy, and unconditional love, we got through this hardship. Even in death, the elders in the community will say everything happens for a reason, and we go home when we are supposed to.

When I worked in my home community of Fort Qu'Appelle as a reintegration worker, I came across trying situations. It was a true learning curve in my career. I got to know the youth in community. I was successful in working with the youth and had positive experiences. Although I maintained professionalism with them, I was sometimes sought out as an auntie figure. The youth I worked with would tell me their background, and I was to be there for them as support. I encouraged them to make positive choices, and a lot of teachings from my younger years came flooding back. I could hear the words of my parents, grandparents, and elders. These teachings became my philosophy in my work. I also learned that positive change usually happens in small steps.

During my years as a reintegration worker, I unfortunately had two of my youth pass away. It was so heartbreaking and sad. I felt as though I had failed. I was engulfed in such guilt because I felt I could have done more in some way. However, with those losses, I learned how precious our youth and children are and the importance of supporting others. At one of the youth's funeral, I saw a line of young people whom I was working with at the time. Seeing me there, they saw me in a different light, and I knew that it was more than a job for me; I was invested in them. That experience changed me and reminded me of the preciousness of life. I always take time to speak to youth when given any opportunity.

THEY ARE TEACHERS TOO

Being an auntie brings me a form of joy and allows me to see my growth. I am never done with growing, nor do I feel that I am at my best. There is always room for a better sense of self. Being an auntie allows me to reflect and share in what life lessons

I have been given, which I hope that other young people won't have to experience. I wasn't always this person people see today. I myself have lived through many of life's lessons, some of which I was not so fond of; others were so beautiful that I needed to share them. Speaking with youth also gives me an opportunity to learn from them just as much as they learn from me. It's a gift and a blessing to be that important person in their world. I love hearing their laughter, their crazy responses, and seeing their continuous curiosity of life. I am blessed to have such beautiful nieces and nephews in this life, and I am proud to be called an auntie. Within Indigenous communities, everyone has the responsibility of ensuring their role is met to create a positively balanced community.

I thought it was important to remember my humble beginnings of becoming an auntie. It amazes me looking back on that distant memory of what I knew then to what I know now. There has been a simple growth into my maturity though the lessons I was given at different turns in events in my life. I feel that I am blessed and wouldn't change these precious moments. There are good, bad, ugly, and, sometimes, unbearable memories, but I can see clearly that I'm making progress. I take time now to thank the Creator for those moments, whether good or bad, as I see them as life lessons. Through it all, the role of being an auntie has become a role that I hold near and dear to my foundation. Each of my nieces and nephews has brought so much light into my world, and they have imprinted on my heart. This chapter is for each of you.

WHAT IS AN AUNTIE?

The honour of being an auntie within Indigenous culture brings many challenges and plays an important role within the family structure. Typically, aunt refers to the sister of one's father or mother or the wife of one's uncle, whereas, informally, the term can be used for an unrelated older woman friend, especially by a child. The importance of being an auntie within Indigenous culture in modern times is to be a positive role model for others.

An auntie is a reliable person that youth or children can go to for advice on many different topics; she is someone who can provide a new perspective on the issues at hand. An auntie can mediate and help both the parents and children come to a mutual understanding, and can provide a form of security and manageable understanding for both parents and children. She is one of the primary role models in the children's life, next to their parents or caregivers. She is a female role model who provides unconditional love, truth, respect, understanding, and endless happiness for younger relatives. I am truly honoured to have the role of being an auntie. All roles and responsibilities build a solid foundation of community bonds.

THE BONDS WE BUILD LAST A LIFETIME

I have stressed throughout this chapter the importance of building positive relationships. I have always felt that I should be that person whom I needed when I was younger. So I became that person. I went through many life lessons. Despite all odds, I ended up back at the teachings of my grandfather. He's been gone for many years, having passed away 28 May 2009. Without him, I felt hopeless and lost. I thought that when I lost him, I lost everything. But he remains my greatest teacher even after death. His messages remain clear and his words strong. In all scenarios and life events, I feel his spirit close by. His guiding words help me through the good, the bad, and everything in between. Resiliency is a powerful tool to use when faced with the challenges of life. I give thanks for taking that time with him while he was around. I learned many wonderful things, and I do my best to honour the bond I had with him. I often find myself sharing his knowledge with those willing to listen. I offer words of love, compassion, and understanding to all my relations.

I know and feel that every bond we build serves a purpose in the life we lead. The importance of surrounding yourself with people who love, respect, support, and push you to be your best self is a revolutionary experience for greater good. It is life changing. It embodies the strength of community and growth, and builds a lifetime of vibrant purpose while honouring the ancestors before you.

A NEW CHAPTER, A FRESH START

Life is a journey in search of truth, understanding, compassion, love, and respect. Although my favourite role is to be an auntie, my new chapter and fresh start is to begin to build the foundation for having a family of my own. I am blessed to have crossed paths with my friend Celina Pelletier. Both two spirited and both female, our relationship provides a lot of strength. We have moments of frustration and disagreement like all others who walk this earth, but overall, I wouldn't change my path for anything. I find peace and happiness with her in my life. I have faced difficult challenges, but now I am ready to put to rest my feelings of fear. I want to embark on a new journey to become a mother. I have found a friend to walk the world with. Life's journey has given me hope and has fostered positive change. I can breathe and stand tall. I can walk this world without fear or shame. I am grateful every day for all the many blessings that I have been given. Thank you Celina for giving me a shoulder to cry on when I needed it and the strength to continue on when I feel that life is too hard. Thank you for loving me when I couldn't face myself. Thank you for believing in me. I love you Celina. I pray that together when we receive blessings to begin our own family we will parent with sincerity and honour. Life's purpose is in the strengths and weaknesses, and is found through truth, understanding, compassion, love, and respect for one another.

CONCLUSION

Overall, I am here pushing forward. I am not perfect but perfectly human with all my life lessons. Creator kept his promise and helped me on my journey. The Creator ensured I would have love, support, truth, and understanding. I keep faith and keep moving forward. Every day, I give thanks for the little things in life and the larger picture. I am grateful and honoured to have this gift of life. I share these teachings given to me. I continue on my path with every step moving in a forward motion. Just like that bus I first took to Vermillion, Alberta, it is constantly moving. I continuously change. Even when life takes me a few steps back or knocks me down, I get up. It is with the ancestral knowledge coursing through my veins that I move forward. I love deeply, I cry, I feel, and I continue to walk forward, a spiritual being. Not perfect, not still, but beautifully an Indigenous auntie. These are words I wish to share with all those reading:

Be careful for each step you take, the children are watching your every move for they might follow you. Make a good path. Make sure the foundation is strong and respectful. Continue on with wisdom and guidance. Gift those young ones with happiness and good words. Love strongly and deeply. Keep moving forward. If you look back, only look back to see how far you have come. Keep going on, celebrate those before, and celebrate those after you. You are a gift. Keep going on.

THANK YOU

I would like to thank those who asked me to be a part of such a beautiful book. I dedicate this chapter to all my nieces and nephews. I love you all equally. Each of you is a blessing in my life. Thank you Creator for life and the lessons therein. Thank you to my partner, mentors, parents, grandparents, sister, siblings, and all adopted relatives across Mother Earth. I am forever grateful for your many teachings and continued support.

Respectfully,

"Ô-ê-*yâh wâkân wî*" Sacred Voice Woman

WORKS CITED

Acoose, Janice. *Iskwewak kah' ki way ni wahkomakanak – Neither Indian Princess nor Easy Squaws*. Women's Press, 1995.

Green, Joyce. *Making space for Indigenous Feminism*. Zed Books Ltd., 2007.

6.
I Am a Metis Mother

TARA TURNER

IT IS HARD TO WRITE about mothering in the midst of actually mothering. It is hard for me to write about being a Metis mother. What do I know about mothering or about being a Metis mother? I am Metis, and I am a mother of three boys, that much I do know. I am a good mother, most of the time, but not a great one, I am sure. I have never thought of myself as a traditional person in any way. I think of myself as Metis, not Métis, with my English roots, but I hear all the discussions about who is Metis and who is not as I write these words. These help feed my fears about writing about Metis mothering. Yet I want to read Metis mother stories to hear how other Metis women navigate being a mother, working, and understand their culture and their lives. So by way of contributing to the conversation, I write.

I have fasted. I have attended ceremonies. I have been to sweat lodges, to pipe ceremonies, and to Grandmother Moon ceremonies. I feel a deep connection to ceremony and to the beliefs and the culture that guide them. I have never been able to solidify for myself a belief in a Creator. I attend ceremonies and smudge still, when it is offered, or I feel the need for it. I feel my culture infused through my life and my world, and I feel fortunate to be able to choose to live my Metis culture in my own way.

I am a person who has a sense of spirituality. I feel connected to the entire world; I talk to my horses; I talk to the moon. I give thanks for our water, our earth, our trees, all the creatures that live here with us. My children know they are Metis. I tell them they are Metis; we read Metis stories, we go to the Batoche festival, and I will include them in my Metis life and culture as we grow together. I teach them the things that I think are important, like all parents do, and I will teach them about their ancestry. I tell them that we are all just humans trying to be our best in this life. I will teach them about relationships with all things in our universe. I will teach them the importance of kindness and being humble. I will teach them about their Metis identity and how this is an important part of who they are. I will teach them respect and understanding for cultural diversity and diversity in all forms. I hope to teach them what I know and how I think while knowing they will choose what they know and think for themselves.

BEING MOTHERED

I knew my family had Metis roots fairly early on, as my mother discovered the connections and gathered the documents and the records from my father's side of the family. Until very recently, she was unable to make the connection in her own family to Metis ancestors, but now she has. This gathering of history is one of the great gifts my mother has given me and my family. Even with my genealogy, and the word Metis, I did not know what it meant for me. Like many Metis people, I did not grow up in a Metis community. When I was young, if I spoke about my heritage at all, I would say that I was part Indian or part Native. In grade school, I remember being called "chief" because of my admission. I felt proud and ashamed of my background. Comments about how I did not look Indian or questions about my blood quantum would silence me and make me feel ashamed of my lack of knowledge and cultural connection. I could feel the racism connected to the comments and questions. I never knew how to respond. Mostly, I kept quiet.

I am fortunate to have come from a home that gave me stability. My mother and my father love me and my siblings. They have always said they love us, and there has never been a moment where that has not felt true and real. My parents are both still alive and still together. They are still in love, and they still treat each of their four children like their little babies that they love so much. My home was a safe place. I had food, clothing, and love. I grew up in a small community, Wynndel, in the Kootenay region of British Columbia. Our house, which my father built for us, was on the lower slope of a mountain and overlooked the Wynndel flats. It was a beautiful place to grow up, with lush green views, and mountain-fed, ice-cold, crystal-clear creeks, rivers, and lakes all around us. It was, and remains, isolated and beautiful. I lived within walking distance of my best friend. Our mothers met during their pregnancies with us. We are still friends and are both now mothers. Our parents are all still alive, still together. We had relatives nearby and neighbourhood people who treated us as special beings and watched out for us, invited us in for food and a drink, and kept an eye on us when we tramped from school to the local swimming pool or when we rode our ponies—mostly too fast. We earned spending money picking strawberries at a local farm. We had horses, dogs, cats, chickens, and chores. We had a large garden, fresh fruit, and a pantry full of canned and frozen food. The acre we lived on seemed a large place and playground to explore. These were my formative years and experiences. The lack of trauma from my childhood is something I now understand as a gift, and one I do not take for granted.

My parents, though, did not have easy lives as children. One of the things that is so remarkable about them is how they found each other and found their way through to providing us with a safe and secure place to grow from. My father's parents were killed in a car accident when he was eight years old. My dad and his four siblings found themselves in an orphanage, and then in the foster care system. Soon the two youngest children were adopted into separate homes and were out of reach and contact with their older siblings. My mother's life was also chaotic, with few constants, and lacked safety and security. I know my parents made many of their choices based on providing a safe and secure home and childhood for me and my siblings. I am grateful to them and all they have done to provide me with a base from which to live a good life and to parent my own children.

Even with this strong base, I spent time rebelling and partying, and I dropped out of high school after barely passing grade ten. After a while, my life settled, and with my mother's encouragement, I ended up in college in Alberta, where I had moved with my partner John. I completed my grade twelve and then a year of university transfer courses. In the library stacks at college, I found and read Maria Campbell's book *Half-breed.* I loved and identified with her story, but I also felt distant from her experience, as my life was so different than hers. Her story stayed with me as I moved along in my education. I did not expect to do so well in school, but I did, and I decided to go on and get a bachelor's degree at the University of Lethbridge. I completed my four-year degree in three years with great distinction. My focus was psychology, but I spent a lot of time in Native studies and with the Native Student Society. I met and spent time with other Indigenous students. I met Ovide Mercredi when he was there giving lectures and presentations. My Introduction to Native Studies professor, who was First Nations, said that the Metis did not exist as a people or a culture, and that Michif was not a language. Another student told me that the Metis were the reason that the buffalo were all gone. This was confusing and hurtful, and I still had no good way to respond. I cried in private. I struggled to understand colonization and decolonization, and how in the world it could relate to me. For an essay, I found the word "diatribe" in my thesaurus and used it to dismiss the writings of Howard Adams about Metis people and their experiences in Canada.

For the first few years of graduate school in clinical psychology, I stayed away from wanting to learn more about my culture and immersed myself in my program with my graduate school peers. There were other Metis students, but it seemed like we would only talk about being Metis to one another, not publicly. And like many other Indigenous students, I was the first in my family to attend university, and there was so much I did not know about it. Although it was not a straightforward journey, I am also one of the many people who have gained knowledge and experiences regarding their cultures while in university, and I am grateful for the opportunities that I have encountered.

MY METIS MOTHERING JOURNEY

I never planned on having children of my own. I did not babysit to earn money as a teenager; instead, I trained ponies and worked as a dishwasher. I did not hold babies—even at baby showers—and I did not understand why people felt children were so charming. They just seemed time consuming and messy to me. And it turns out, I was right, they are. But at thirty-four, I had completed all the requirements of my PhD program other than my dissertation, and I found myself thinking about the possibility of having a family. John is four years older than I am, and has always said he wanted to have children someday. Despite not feeling any particular pull to become a mother, I was starting to think that if we did not try to have a family soon, it would be too late. I heard and read stories of people who tried to conceive for years.

My friend Rose was leading Grandmother Moon ceremonies, and I began to join her at them. I do not remember exactly why I started attending these ceremonies, other than that I knew Rose, and she was leading them, and invited me. At these ceremonies, there was a focus on women, on their strengths, on their gifts, on their roles. I had not often thought of any of these things. My moon time was always just something to be tolerated; being a woman was just what I was. I was not particularly spiritual, and I felt a long way from sorting that out. At these Grandmother Moon ceremonies, in the comfort and company of these women, and after when we sat together and talked and ate and laughed and cried, I felt myself softening and thinking about being a woman and my role as a woman in a new way. My friend Tania, who has four kids, kept trying to convince me to start a family. She said if I decided that I did not like the baby, I could give it to her.

I was working on my dissertation on Metis identity when I became pregnant with my first child. There were so many things I thought about and worried about during that pregnancy, and since I was deep into my dissertation, identity was one of them. My dissertation research was focused on Metis identity precisely because I found it so tricky, troubling, and painful. I spent much of my life not having answers to the questions I would ask myself such as, why did I care about being Metis?

I was searching for answers with my dissertation and with my father and his brothers and sisters, who joined my research journey as participants. Their connection to their family, and their father's Metis culture, was broken when six people from their family, including their parents, died all in less than one year. Their aunt Jenny died on Christmas Eve of 1954, their grandmother died on New Year's Eve of that same year, and their grandfather died a month later on the last day of January in 1955. Their parents died in a car accident on 30 July 1955, the accident also took the life of their unborn sibling who was due to be born any day.

My father and his brothers and sisters were ultimately separated from one another, and all ended up in the system in different ways. The oldest three—Judy, Bob, and Ed—never lost touch with one another, and all except the youngest, Debbie, were placed in the same orphanage about a year after their parents' deaths. Debbie was placed for adoption less than a year after the accident, and was moved from her aunt's place to her adoptive home without her sibling's knowledge. Brian, the second youngest, spent about a year in the orphanage with his siblings before also being placed in an adoptive home, again without being able to say goodbye to his siblings, even though they were in the same orphanage. Brian and Debbie were adopted out individually, but not as siblings together—they were adopted as white children, with no acknowledgement of their Metis heritage. The oldest three were in orphanage longer, and then each lived in a couple of foster homes.

I thought of the stories my father shared with me, starting when I was a child. He would tell me about what he remembered when his family was together. He told me about his grandmother and her beautiful beaded gauntlet gloves, and the bearskin rug in her room. He remembered what a great shot she was. He talked about his grandfather and how kind he was, how he spoke Cree to him and his siblings, and how he nicknamed him *Wopastikwin*, little white head, as my father was so blond when he was a child. My father remembered that his family, the Turners, was known as "half-breeds" in Fort Saskatchewan and how his mother's family was English and not pleased with the marriage of their daughter to this half-breed man. His aunt Jenny collected medicines. His family and their relatives would gather on occasions, and there would be music, dancing, food and drink. My dad clearly loved his grandparents and his parents. His parents and grandparents clearly loved their children and grandchildren.

I remember pictures of my father's parents that were in a picture frame that hung in our house. Their images were captured separately as they posed in a rocking chair in their house. I would look at them and try and imagine them as real people. My grandmother's name was Winnie, and loving horses, I loved that name. It was hard as a child to feel connected to them. Their presence was their constant absence in my life. My dad does not remember conversations with his parents, just snippets, like his mom's face, and that she used to put icing sugar on bread as a treat for the kids. He does not remember talks with his dad either but remembers events, like how his dad took the kids up to the roof of the house to watch the fireworks at exhibition time in Edmonton. He remembers his house. He remembers the night that his parents died, that people came to his house, including his mother's sister, and that they told the kids that their parents had died. He says he does not remember feeling anything or anyone talking to them about what happened—it was "just kind of a blur." His stories do not often revolve around remembrances of his parents, but of his time at his uncles after the accident, playing with his cousins and being in the orphanage and foster care.

They found each other, my father and his siblings, and were eventually reunited. Through my dissertation, gathering their stories and bringing them together to share and record their stories, I gained a great deal of understanding and peace about this part of my father's life and my own history. Although my father told me good and happy stories about his time growing up, I think the enormity of the losses always felt more significant to me, even as I began my dissertation. But during my time with my father and his brothers and sisters, I found a strong and loving family, people who love each other and their own families. They have good lives, and they are good people. They each have their own understanding of their Metis ancestry.

It is through having my own children that I have come to fully understand my father's family story and the impact and resonance of their experiences. Alexander, my oldest son, is now eight. He is the same age as my father was when his parents died. I wonder what Alexander would remember about his parents if we were gone from his world. When Alexander turned one, I thought of my auntie Debbie and how it was her first birthday when her world changed—how she was moved to the home of one of her relatives, without her siblings, and probably without any understanding of what was happening and why. As each of my children moved through that stage, I have thought of that and of the confusion, fear, and anxiety that my auntie would have experienced. The same is true of my fears and feelings when each of my boys was the age of my uncle Brian, who was three when his parents died—the age of my son Weston now. My uncle Brian was four when he was taken from the orphanage, without getting to say goodbye to any of his siblings. My son Sebastian is four. My uncle Bob was eleven and my auntie Judy was thirteen when they lost their parents. I know these stages and ages are coming up with my children soon. Seeing my children at these different ages means experiencing the pain and the joy with the heart of a mother and as a daughter.

In the years since I finished my dissertation and since becoming a mother, so much has changed in my life and my thoughts. I know that it was not my family's choice to be wrenched from their culture. I know that any or all of us can pick it up and learn Metis culture for ourselves in ways that make sense to us and resonate with who we are at the moment. I am fortunate now to have access to Metis people, places, and culture, and I want that for my whole family, including my children. I think all Metis people who have been separated from their families and their culture need access to ways to understand themselves as Metis people.

I do wonder and worry whether I should have created more of a Metis community for my kids. Will I regret not having ceremonies for them when they were little? I worry about what they will learn about the Metis culture and First Nations culture in schools. What will their peers and their friends say about First Nations and Metis people? How will they react to and navigate through racism? Will some of them choose to identify as Metis and learn to follow their culture? Will others will not? How will I feel if they do not identify as Metis? They are all so fair skinned and light eyed. It is easy for me to remember the uncertainty I had about being Metis when I was young, and I do not want that for my children. I know my children will also have these kinds of experiences and that they will come from strangers and from people they care about. They will be hurt by them. They will hear racist comments about First Nations and Metis people in situations where they are seen as white. They will have to decide if they are going to speak up or remain silent. I will try to give them all the connection and words that they need to feel the strength to always speak up and to know their Metis culture. I will love them through whatever choices they make for themselves. I never want them to feel shame because they are Metis. I hope they never do.

I AM A MOTHER

It still feels strange sometimes to know that I am a mother. I think about how I have replicated my childhood in many ways; the childhood that I thought was so boring as I approached my teenage years. My children are loved, and they know they are loved. I tell them that I love them every time I think it. I hug, kiss, and cuddle with them as much as they can stand it. I want them to feel cherished. They are growing up with a parent at home. They have room to roam on our acreage, animals to love and learn from, and a significant lack of technology and pop culture.

Being a mother is the hardest thing ever, harder than anything else. It is rewarding, and I love my kids in a way that I never could have imagined that I would. I love babies and kids now—my own and others. It has all been a surprise for me. Describing the experience of motherhood is individual and particular. It is always changing, always true and real. Being a mother, for me, has eclipsed all previous experiences I have had. I hate being a mother too, often enough. It is hard, endless, relentless, and exhausting. I am tired in ways and to levels that I did not even dream possible. But how I love them is amazing to me. They help me in my life. My children force me to have more balance. To know more easily that my work is only one part of my life, not the most important part. Work is not what defines me, and it is not the judge of my worth—my family is and my children are. They are who I am accountable to. I am so grateful for that, for them, and for what they give to me without even knowing it.

Before I had my children, and early in my PhD process, I remember meeting with Maria Campbell to talk to her about my dissertation and my research. I expressed to her my deepest fears, about how I never felt like I was Metis—at least not in the way that she was. I did not know how to write a dissertation about Metis identity out of a family story that felt fragmented, full of pain, and lacking in culture in any way besides genealogy and documents. Maria heard me, and she talked to me about how culture is more than one thing, that it is not just being from a Metis community, or knowing the language, or attending ceremonies. She said it is also about being good people, caring about each other and for each other, and about being kind and being a family. I remember feeling understood, cared for, and validated in that exchange. I felt that I could begin the process of laying down my fears and uncertainties about my family and my identity and just get on with the work of collecting our stories.

We all know how important stories are to Metis culture. It took me a long time to understand that my family had a Metis story of its own. I grew up looking for the Metis parts to my family story. I know now that our whole story, including the past and the time we are living now, is a Metis story. It is our story, our Metis family story, and it is a good, strong story. I am glad that I have found my way to this place, this Metis space, for me, my family, and my children. I learned a lot about myself and my culture over the years. As for being a Metis mother, there is much more to know, and there always will be. But I know as much as I can for now. I know who I am now, and I know that might change. I know that is just fine, as it all part of my story.

WORKS CITED

Campbell, Marie. *Half-breed*. Goodread Biographies,1973.

7.
Mother Earth, Mother Mine, Mother Me, Mother Time

ELDER BETTY MCKENNA

MOTHERING, OR MOTHER EARTH nurturing, is a term the old ones used and one I prefer; mothering (Mother Earth nurturing) starts before the day we are born—right from the moment of the first spark of life, we are able to taste, smell, feel, and hear nurturing. The water surrounding us in the womb nurtures us. How could one not know nurturing? The old ones used to say mothering is in our bones—our ways of mothering are strong. It's the root that binds us all to Mother Earth. Of course, roots wither without nourishment from Mother Earth, and the roots of Mother Earth nurturing withered for my people through colonization and all the ills that came with that process.

Roots revive themselves, and so too it was within our people: tribe by tribe, woman by woman, and man by man. Families began to repair, to share, and to develop new ways and understandings of the Creator's gift of life through ceremony. They pass it to the boys, who as men are able to realize their own ways of mothering, whereas our warriors will come full circle so that mothering will once again not be separated by gender. Then, once again, the circle of Mother Earth nurturing will encompass the child by incorporating all things—all the presences of spirit and beings who contribute in the welcoming of the child through the doorway from the spirit world into the physical realm.

MY BIRTH

I was there but remember none of it. My mother said I woke her sometime after 3:00 a.m. and was born at 4:00 a.m. I was her fourth child and second daughter. I still wake at 4:00 a.m. every day, and I really have no idea why. There is nothing going on at that time of day. But I pray, sit, and listen. The ancestors are close by; I feel humbled that they grace me with their presence. I feel heavy when they leave.

MY CHILDHOOD TEACHERS

I grew up watching, listening. My teachers were my grandmothers, mother, and my aunts. Every gesture, glance, and nod of head was a unique means of communication, which over the generations my people have not forgotten. They belong to a language that was gentle and soft—no words to break the spell of quiet and sunlight. I would sit on the floor and gaze at them not knowing that it was a world my children would never experience.

Whenever my siblings and I would try something new, we would watch and listen to our dad, grandpa, and uncles. They would caution us to "take your time" and to "give it a chance," as we "might like it." With flashing eyes and grins, they willed us through our struggles, and as my dad would say to us, "there are no girls' or boys' jobs, just jobs." We learned to do them all, and we did—my sisters, my brothers, and I.

I never heard any complaints from my family, just lots of laughter. I loved mom and dad's stories told on a cold winter afternoon; their family history was full of adventure and hardship. My ancestors emerged from those stories before my eyes—humble, proud, hardworking, and with centuries of resilience.

MY LAND

I am from Mother Earth. I am her child, the one created from moose meat and blueberries. She calls the older sisters and brothers to help me understand her messages of colour, smell, and sound. Plants, trees, and flowers have their own form of communication, and it's the same as my mom's and my aunties' form of communication, gentle and soft.

The wind, rain, and snow drive you through the struggle of each season. The struggles we face each season as humans—physically, mentally, spiritually, and emotionally from childhood to old age—help us to find our place. Sometimes one likes it and sometimes one finds that liking it or not you have made it to the next season. There are no girls' seasons or boys' seasons, just seasons, and we learn to live through them all.

We have lived here forever, and Mother Earth has created us from the iron, zinc, potassium, salt, and copper that lay within her, and our siblings, the rocks and stones, are the first children that laboured to keep us well as we walked upon our mother. We were taught that this is the way we nurture: to never give up on the weakest or the youngest. We may moan and groan, but if we allow laughter to help us through our toughest times, our load can be lightened. In everything that we do, someone is watching. We teach with our lives, we live with the breath, and we take with the words when we speak our actions—however we do it, someone will follow if we teach earnestly. That someone who watches me will live earnestly, and if I teach tolerance and love that someone who watches me will blossom in life.

UNCONDITIONAL LOVE

Unconditional love is a phrase you hear connected to nurturing in a mothering way. It should be that with life, I love all things unconditionally—every person, animal, plant, and tree. Unconditional means to accept things because they exist. It's not like saying I only love that plant because it smells good or has a pretty flower on it. I love it and place no conditions on that plant in order to love it; I just do. It works the same way with humans: "I love you because you are in the world."

HOW I GATHERED AND BLOSSOMED IN LIFE

I had no barriers in my childhood. I hauled snow and water. I split wood, sawed wood, and hauled wood so that I could cook and bake. I paddled a canoe, fished, and set rabbit snares, skinned rabbits, and made soup: When I grew up, no one said you're a girl and girls do not do that. Instead, I was praised for my eagerness to learn and work so that I felt valued and needed. I was given choices as a child; however, I was told you can learn how to sew or learn how to knit, but you will learn one of them. Doing nothing was not an option, and I learned that having a skill gave me status among my peers.

The first thing I would like young mothers and fathers to know is that your child is not your friend and they should never be your friend. The child and parent should have an open and trusting relationship, with each having their own friends. I know many teens who tell me how their father or mother claims they are their best friend. Well, all I can say is, stop it people! It scares the hell out of them. How do I know? They come to me for help about it. Kids won't tell their parents that speaking in this manner makes them fearful. They go along with it and say the things that their parents want them to say. Why? Because maybe, just maybe, they fear their parents will stop loving them. They feel that that there is a condition placed on them to play the role of a friend for an insecure parent.

My mother and father were not my friends. They loved me more than any friend, and they prepared me for life without them. I have done the same for my children. Nor were my grandmothers my friends; instead, they prepared my mind for the future regularly and repetitively shared the knowledge they gave me to carry. And never once did they say, "I told you that already," and nor did they ask, "how many times do you have to be told?" They never said I made mistakes; instead they said I gave myself another opportunity to do it again in another way. Competition was explained and demonstrated to me as something you do with yourself. If I carried four armloads of wood one day, I could compete with myself and bring in five armloads the next day. And every time I carried wood or water, my grandmother would say I was helping my bones to be strong just as when I ate the bone marrow that helped build my bones. I go through life now competing with myself every day. I have given that gift of competition to my grandson and granddaughter. I watch them face each new day with a zest for the challenges that this life offers while they strive to better themselves.

Happiness is a choice. The old ones used to say, "If you make plans, for instance to go for a walk and it rains, you can happily go anyway or happily stay home and talk about rain and its blessing." Sadness, on the other hand, is to be shared, especially over a cup of sweet tea. My grandmother used to say, "the more you cry the less you pee." My other grandmother used to say, "no one ever died from crying." She also would say let them suck their thumb, since they can't swallow it. I loved my grandmothers early-morning visits bringing, as they did, the smell of tanned moose hide and rose water. Discipline means to teach and if you can't talk it into someone, you can't beat it into someone. Therefore, we should talk less and hug often—a practice that has held me steadfast through the challenging rapids of life with my own three children. The rapids of life are those sacred years from thirteen to nineteen. They are the years when we look for missing seven stones in our life: growth, order, adequacy, love, security, social approval, and self-esteem.

Ceremony gives us these stones. There are many ceremonies: water ceremonies, fasting ceremonies, feasting ceremonies, smudging ceremonies, picking medicine and berry ceremonies, and naming ceremonies; sweat lodge, moon lodge, and Grandmother Moon ceremonies; story ceremonies, pipe ceremonies, rock ceremonies, sunrise ceremonies, and shaky tent ceremonies. There are many more I have not named, and they are all nurturing, safe, and gentle. They cover one's life from birth to death and after.

Every nation has their differences as to the why and what of this ceremony, and they may differ from community to community. I have participated in many different smudging ceremonies and when I tell the young ones why and how to smudge I always go back to my roots. For example, sage is picked in ceremony, while we offer tobacco when it is ready to be picked. There are different kinds of sage, such as white sage, pasture sage, female sage, and male sage, to name a few. After picking, the sage is laid out to dry, if it is the broad leafed female sage. Others can be bundled into bunches, tied, and hung to dry. After it's dry, I roll it into a small ball in the palm of my hand place it in an abalone shell and light it once. As the smoke rises, I wash it over my head and as I wash it over me, I think good thoughts. I wash the smoke over my eyes to see good things, over my ears to hear good things, over my mouth to say good things, over my heart to feel good things, and then down to Mother Earth for holding me as I pray.

MAKING MOTHERS

Once a young girl is on the verge of her first moon time, she is encouraged to fulfill the berry fast ceremony. During this fast, she cannot eat berries for one year. The Berry Fast Ceremony teaches a girl to delay self-gratification, which is a valued traditional skill for young women. The Berry Fast Ceremony is important to young girls, and during this ceremony, a girl's grandmother prepares her white ceremonial dress, while her hair is braided with red willow. This ceremony takes place during a full moon, wherein a grandmother leads her granddaughter to a place beside the sacred fire and the girl's mother comes and sits with her for strength and support. Her aunts stand in the four directions with the one in the East holding strawberries, the one in the West holding Saskatoon berries, the one in the South holding raspberries, and the one in the North holding blueberries. One by one, the girl is approached by her aunts and offered berries, which she feeds on until she no longer wants any. She is offered berries four times, and each time, she is told that this is the last taste of berries for a year. When she can no longer eat, she bids her sister berries to stay well, as she will hold them in her heart and memory until the next year when she is once again allowed to break her fast and eat berries. The girl then has red ocher marked on her feet and hands to seal her promise to her sister berry.

There is also the Full Moon Ceremony, and once Grandmother Moon is full, people gather to honour her and the role she plays in our lives, and the water within us and without. The Full Moon Ceremony is different from the Moon Time Ceremony, which is held on the ninth moon and is the moon that women learn women's teachings. The Full Moon Ceremony has general teachings that men and young boys learn along with mothers, grandmothers, sisters, aunties, and daughters.

During ceremony, we sing songs and drum. A sacred fire is lit, and tobacco ties are burned while some people burn their cut hair in a cloth hair bundle. We also burn sage and cedar and after the closing with prayer and travelling songs, we all share food and tea. I also do pipe ceremonies but I don't use tobacco in my pipe, and the sweats I conduct are from the bear spirit, and naming ceremonies and sunrise ceremonies are also ones I conduct. At this time, the grandmothers and grandfathers have not instructed me in the way to put the above mentioned ceremonies on paper so I won't, but I will say this that if you are ever in my neck of the woods, look me up and you can attend a ceremony. It's the best way to find out about them, and everyone is welcome.

About the Contributors

Carrie Bourassa is the Chair of Northern & Indigenous Health at Health Sciences North Research Institute and the scientific director of the Institute of Aboriginal Peoples' Health at the Canadian Institutes of Health Research. Prior to her recent appointments in October 2016 and February 2017 respectively, Dr. Bourassa served as an Indigenous community-based researcher for the past sixteen years at First Nations University of Canada as a professor of Indigenous health studies. Carrie's research interests include the impacts of colonization on the health of Indigenous people; creating culturally safe care in health service delivery; and Indigenous community-based health research methodology. Carrie is Métis, belonging to the Regina Riel Métis Council #34.

Nancy Cooper is Anishinaabe from the Chippewas of Rama First Nation in southern Ontario. Born and raised in northern Ontario, Nancy is an adult educator and an artist. She has spent her career working in her community while her graduate thesis focused on the transformative nature of culture-based literacy provision. Nancy is a published author whose work can be found in edited anthologies, such as *Me Sexy* (2008) and *The Colour of Resistance* (1994). She is also the author of several adult literacy publications for Ningwakwe Learning Press, such as *Journeys of the Spirit* (2013). Nancy is a mom of twin boys and so honoured that these two complex beings chose her.

Leah Marie Dorion is a self-taught Indigenous (Metis) interdisciplinary artist and writer from Prince Albert, Saskatchewan, Canada. She is a respected children's book writer and several of her books have been nominated for various awards for their art and cultural content. For more information visit www.leahdorion.ca; email: leahdorionart@gmail.com.

Darlene M. Juschka teaches in women's and gender studies and religious studies at the University of Regina. Her areas of interest are semiotics, feminisms, and posthumanism. Some of her more recent work include: "Feminism and Gender" in *The Oxford Handbook of the Study of Religion* (2016); with Melissa Wuerch, Kim Zorn, and Mary Hampton "Responding to Intimate Partner Violence: Challenges Faced among Service Providers in Northern Communities" (2016); and "Enfleshing Semiotics: TheIndexical and Symbolic Sign-Functions" (2014). She has also published two texts; *Political Bodies, Body Politic: The Semiotics of Gender* (2014; 2009) and *Feminism in the Study of Religion: A Reader* (2001).

Elder Betty McKenna is Anishnabae from the Shoal River Band #366 who, with her husband Ken, has had three children. She is an elder for First Nations and Métis education at the Regina Public School Board, a lecturer of Indigenous Health Studies in social work and biology, and guiding elder for many research projects, including research and education for solutions to violence and abuse. She has co-authored several peer-reviewed publications and has served on the College of Physicians and Surgeons and National Elders Advisory Corrections Canada. Elder Betty was the recipient of the Queen's Gold and Diamond Jubilee medals and Excellence in Health award.

Paulete Poitras is a Dakota/Cree from Muscowpetung First Nation. She was raised with culturally enriched values of both positive morals and ethics and is thirty-one years of age living a sober and healthy lifestyle with her partner Celina Pelletier. She attended Saskatchewan PolyTech and received an applied certificate in Law Enforcement. She has successfully worked four years at File Hills Qu'Appelle Tribal Council in the Justice Department as a youth reintegration worker. Thereafter, she began to work in the field of community-based research in the field of health, where building a healthy community is the goal.

Janet Smylie is a Métis woman, mother of six, family physician, and public health researcher. She currently works as the director of the Well Living House Action Research Centre for Indigenous Infant, Child, and Family Wellbeing at St. Michael's Hospital and an Associate Professor at the Dalla Lana School of Public Health, University of Toronto. She has practised and taught family medicine for over twenty years and maintains a part-time clinical practice at Seventh Generation Midwives Toronto. Dr. Smylie acknowledges her family, lodge, and traditional teachers. She currently holds a CIHR Applied Public Health Chair in Indigenous Health.

Blair Stonechild, PhD, a member of the Muscowpetung First Nation in Saskatchewan, is professor of Indigenous studies at the First Nations University of Canada. An internationally recognized researcher in the fields of Indigenous studies and Indigenous post-secondary education, Dr. Stonechild's work on land claims and higher education for First Nations has created many opportunities and has led to greater awareness of these very important issues. His book *The New Buffalo: The Struggle for Post-Secondary Education* (2006) is considered one of the leading texts in the field.

Tara Turner has a PhD is in clinical psychology from the University of Saskatchewan. Her dissertation is titled "Re-searching Metis Identity: My Metis Family Story." Tara's teaching and research interests include identity, health, motherhood, parenting, family and child welfare, and in applying Indigenous thinking, models, and methods to these areas. Tara lives on acreage with her partner and their three young children. She is an assistant professor at the First Nations University of Canada, Saskatoon Campus, in the School of Indigenous Social Work.